The Civil War's First Blood

A MAP OF THE
ATLANTIC OCEAN
SHOWING THE
AMERICAN & EUROPEAN PORTS
and the
ROUTES OF THE OCEAN STEAMERS

THE
ISTHMUS of PANAMA
showing the
ROUTES OF TRADE BETWEEN
CHAGRES & PANAMA

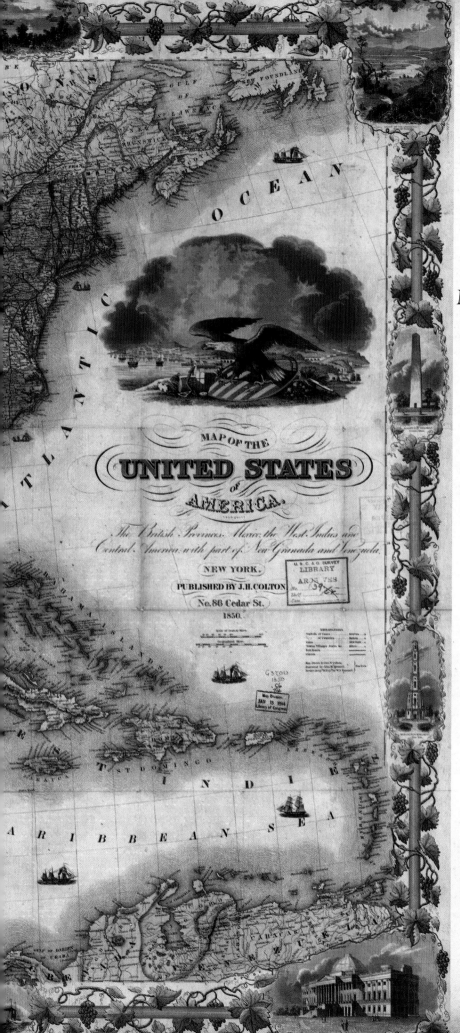

The Civil War's First Blood

MISSOURI 1854–1861

JAMES DENNY
JOHN BRADBURY

Missouri*Life*
Boonville, Missouri
MissouriLife.com

Acknowledgments

The authors would like to thank James E. McGhee for his careful and insightful reading of the entire manuscript and for his unfailing encouragement of this project. Thanks are also due Roger Boyd for his critique of Chapter 6. James Denny would like to dedicate this book to his wife, Susan Denny. She not only contributed her editorial expertise to this project, but also her constant support.

Editor: Rebecca French Smith
Designer: Barbara King

Editorial Director: Danita Allen Wood
Publisher: Greg Wood

Missouri Life, Inc.
515 East Morgan Street
Boonville, Missouri 65233
800-492-2593
MissouriLife.com

Cover: *Battle of Wilson's Creek* by N.C. Wyeth. *Missouri: Capitol, Photographs, 1913-1927, Western Historical Manuscript Collection, Columbia, MO*

Page ii-iii: The United States in 1850 as depicted on a map by J. H. Colton published in New York. *Library of Congress*

Page vi: Map of Missouri as it appeared in 1855 published by J. H. Colton, New York. *Missouri Department of Natural Resources*

Contents

	BEFORE THE WAR	1
Prologue	1861	11
Chapter 1	MISSOURI'S SECESSION CRISIS	14
Chapter 2	THE ROAD TO BOONVILLE	28
Chapter 3	THE BATTLE OF CARTHAGE	39
Chapter 4	THE BATTLE OF WILSON'S CREEK	45
Chapter 5	A TALE OF TWO GOVERNMENTS	56
Chapter 6	CHOOSING SIDES NORTH MISSOURI STYLE	63
Chapter 7	HIGH TIDE FOR THE MISSOURI SOUTHERN CAUSE	73
Chapter 8	THE PATHFINDER'S CURTAIN CALL	87
Chapter 9	CIVIL WAR COMES TO SOUTHEAST MISSOURI	105
Chapter 10	THE TWELFTH CONFEDERATE STATE	115
Chapter 11	PRICE MOVES NORTH AGAIN	126
Conclusion	WHAT THE FUTURE HELD	135

The Civil War's First Blood

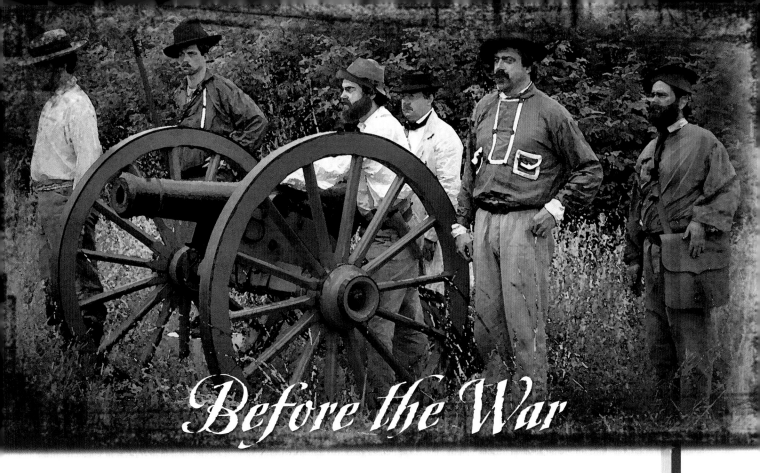

Before the War

IF IT HAD BEEN up to the people of Missouri, the Civil War might never have happened. Few Missourians desired the conflict. If they had had their "druthers," Missouri's citizens would have remained neutral. They were against Missouri's leaving the Union, yet they also firmly opposed any coercing of the Southern states by the North, even when those states severed their connection to the Union.

The desire for neutrality proved unrealistic, and it didn't last long once extremists gained control. When the war began, it immediately engulfed the state and pulled its people into the terrible vortex of civil war. And for all the reluctance of Missourians to become involved, the citizens of no other state, North or South, so experienced the full effects of the conflict that erupted. War showed all its many dreadful faces and nearly destroyed the civic and social structures of Missouri in the process. It spread over all regions of Missouri and wrought every variety of hardship and suffering. Each level of society and every niche and corner of the beleaguered state experienced the escalating harshness of the war. Unfortunately, much of the conflict pitted Missourians against other Missourians. There were no exemptions for neutrals, the aged, women, or children—all came to feel what Gen. William Sherman termed the "hard hand of war."

When the time came to choose sides, Missourians immediately responded. Fighting men in no other state went for their hunting pieces more quickly or with more lethal intent. The initial reluctance on the part of most Missourians to embrace the coming war had nothing to do with pacifism or the lack of a warlike spirit on the part of its citizens. To the contrary, Missourians to that time had never seen a war on American soil they weren't willing to pitch into. Missouri frontiersmen fought the American Indians in the War of 1812 to guarantee their foothold on Missouri soil. Missouri volunteers marched north to join in putting down the uprising of Chief Black Hawk in Illinois and Wisconsin in 1832; five years later, other volunteers

By 1856 the confrontation between Kansas Free Staters and Missouri Southern sympathizers was becoming violent. Free Staters began to build an arsenal that ranged from cannons and accoutrements to cases of rifles, called Beecher's Bibles, shipped west from New England states. *Reenactment photo, Steve Wilson*

Before the Louisiana Purchase, American frontiersmen, such as Daniel Boone, were already flooding into the territory that would become Missouri, often bringing their extended families and slaves with them. *Missouri Historical Society, St. Louis*

Slavery had been a part of Missouri's fabric since French times. By 1860, the state contained 114,509 slaves. As the map shows, most slaves were concentrated in the rich agricultural lands bordering the Missouri River. *"Atlas of Antebellum Southern Agriculture" by Sam Bowers Hilliard, Louisiana State University Press, 1984*

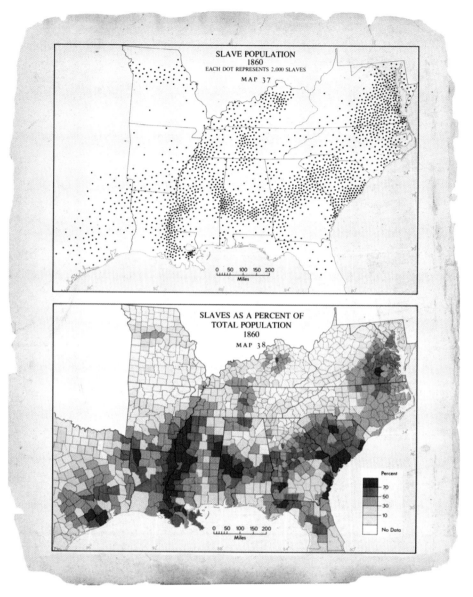

marched south to the swamps of Florida to suppress defiant Seminoles. In 1838, the government of Missouri declared war on the Mormons, who had managed to antagonize their Missouri neighbors thoroughly, and fielded an army to drive them from the state. Between 1846 and 1848, thousands of Missourians made the long trek southwest to defeat Mexico. One Missouri commander captured the quality of that fierce fighting spirit that animated Missourians, "My men fought like hell and whipped everything before them." The Mexican War was an important military training ground for a large number of Missourians who were later to play significant roles in the Civil War.

Despite their profound reluctance to sever ties with the Union, Missourians, who were fundamentally Southern in culture and heritage, constituted the majority of the state's population. Identity with the South was a powerful and pervasive force in Missouri society and politics. Even before the Louisiana Purchase, frontier migrants from the upper South, the most famous being Daniel Boone, crossed the Mississippi to settle in Spanish-controlled upper Louisiana, where they found a well-watered, forested land reminding them of their ancestral homelands in Virginia, Kentucky, and Tennessee. This land was ideally suited to the establishment of Southern agriculture

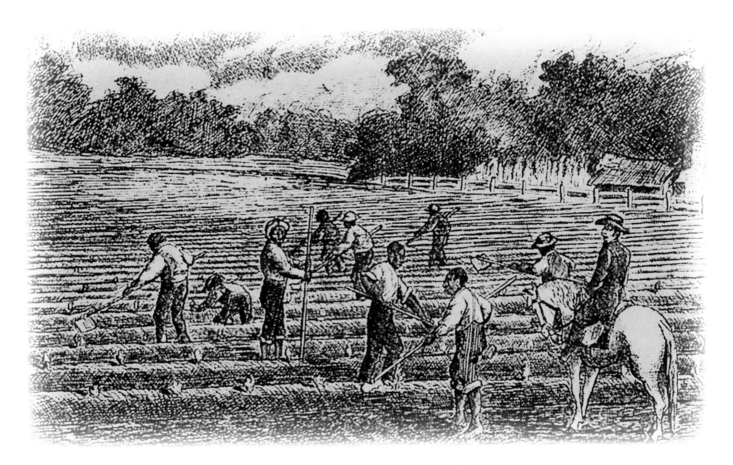

and customs. With the transfer of the region to the United States in 1803, this influx of Southern migrants turned into a tide. Following the War of 1812, it seemed to some observers that whole sections of Kentucky and Tennessee were breaking up and becoming part of the Missouri Territory. By the 1850s, perhaps 75 percent of the population could claim Southern ancestry. Had this whole population block believed in secession, they could have easily carried Missouri out of the Union and into the Confederacy in the opening months of the war.

The French had introduced slavery west of the Mississippi River in the eighteenth century, so Southerners found it easy to transplant their own system of chattel slavery. The institution thrived most in the tiers of counties along either side of the Missouri River and along the Mississippi River, where the agricultural potential made slavery economically viable. By 1860, these counties contained nearly 77 percent of all Missouri's 114,509 slaves.

Missouri's version of Southern slave-based civilization, however, contained little of the "moonlight and magnolias" variety of leisurely plantation living so often associated with the Deep South. Plantations with large gangs of slaves were a rare sight in Missouri—only thirty-eight people in the entire state owned more than fifty slaves. Only one in eight Missouri families owned any slaves at all, and those families owned an average of 4.7 slaves. In the Deep South, half the population owned slaves, averaging 12.7 bondsmen each. It is little wonder that Deep South slaveholders had a consuming devotion to the defense of slavery, which in their eyes was fundamentally a question of property rights rather than the status of the Negro. That passion did not carry over to Missouri with the same fanatical intensity or result in the same universal determination to break the ties of Union.

A Missouri master was more likely to be found working alongside his slaves rather than sitting on the veranda sipping mint juleps. And while tobacco and

Although this image depicts a gang of slaves laboring under the scrutiny of an overseer, most slave owners in Missouri owned fewer than five slaves and often worked in the fields alongside their bondsmen. *Used by permission, State Historical Society of Missouri, Columbia*

hemp were staple crops of the state's plantations, most slaveholders practiced a diversified agriculture that produced huge crops of corn, wheat, and other cereals. There were large herds of cattle, hogs, and sheep, and Missouri was also noted for fine horses and mules. Most Southerners in Missouri could be described as yeoman farmers rather than planters. In the Ozark Highlands region, former residents of Tennessee and other states carried on their traditions of raising stock on open range supplemented by subsistence farming, along with raising enough corn in fertile creek and river bottoms to make cornmeal and whiskey. Ozarkers seldom owned slaves and had little regard for the high-living "bourbons" who did.

The population of slaves grew steadily during the antebellum years, nearly doubling between 1840 and 1860, but this increase did not match that of the white population. Slaves comprised 17.8 percent of the population in 1830, but three decades later, they made up only 9.7 percent. Despite this percentage decline, the institution of slavery exerted a powerful hold on the state's political system. Slaveholders and their worldview held sway in the legislative, judicial, and executive branches of Missouri government throughout the pre-Civil War years. This dominance persisted despite many transformations taking place in Missouri that changed its society and economy.

Southern Americans were hardly the only population element drawn to Missouri. Old World Germans found the state attractive as a place to settle, particularly after the publication in 1827 of Gottfried Duden's *Report of a Journey to the Western States of North America*. It described the lower Missouri River valley as a veritable Rhineland ripe for the establishment of a New Germany. Thousands of Germans poured into Missouri in the pre-Civil War years. By 1860, St. Louis had a German population of fifty thousand, the largest concentration of Germans in any American city. Thousands more settled along the Missouri River in tightly knit communities. Many of these industrious newcomers fled the economic and political upheavals that convulsed Europe in the first half of the nineteenth century. A significant number of the émigrés had fought against reactionary European nobility in the Revolution of 1848 and fled to the New World following their defeat. They brought with them a hatred of aristocracy and tyranny and saw slavery and slaveholders as an extension of the evils they had fled in the Old World. While Southerners wrestled with ambivalent attitudes about secession and union, no such uncertainty troubled German immigrants—they were devout Unionists ready to defend a nation whose language they often could barely speak and to offer their military experience to the cause of freedom in their new fatherland.

These new arrivals were supplemented by an influx of migrants from northern states—a group constituting 15 percent of Missouri's population in 1860. By the outbreak of the Civil War, three in ten Missourians hailed from either the northeastern states or foreign countries. These two groups were the fastest growing components of the state's population.

Economic forces also linked Missouri to northern industrial centers, but there were none more important than railroads. Missouri caught the railroad building mania late. By the time the first mile of track was laid in the state, a network of seven thousand miles of rails connected Chicago, New York, and Boston. In 1859, the completion of the Hannibal and St. Joseph, Missouri's first rail line, linked the state to the extensive transportation network and industrial centers of the North. By 1860, eight hundred miles of railroad had been constructed. St. Louis, the state's largest city and industrial center, had a nascent network of railroads radiating into Missouri's rich agricultural and mineral hinterlands. The St. Louis and Iron Mountain Railroad connected with the rich iron ore regions around Pilot

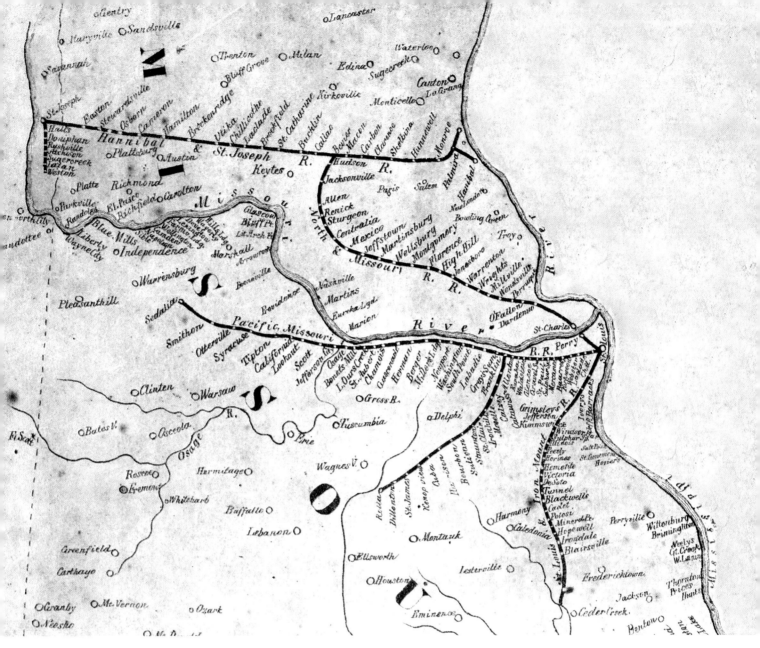

Knob, while the Pacific Railroad of Missouri had been built west through the state capital to the fledgling town of Sedalia. Its branch line, the South West Branch of the Pacific Railroad, was complete as far as Rolla by the end of 1860. The North Missouri Railroad connected St. Louis with the Hannibal and St. Joseph Railroad at Macon.

For all the forces at work to make Missouri a border state with one foot in the South and one in the West, the state played as central a role as any Deep South state in the long-simmering slavery controversy that ultimately erupted in civil war. Indeed, the state's difficult birth spawned the first national crisis over slavery. Missouri's admission as a slave state brought about bitter debate in Congress and resulted in the Missouri Compromise of 1821. The Missouri Compromise held the nation together by maintaining the delicate balance between slave and free states. Missouri was allowed to enter the Union as a slave state at the same time that Maine was admitted as a free state. Part of the Missouri Compromise attempted to address the further spread of slavery, as well, by stipulating that all Louisiana Purchase territory north of the southern boundary of Missouri, except Missouri, would be free, while slavery could exist below the so-called Mason-Dixon line.

The Missouri Compromise was a stopgap measure that preserved the Union

By the time of the Civil War, Missouri had the most extensive rail network of any state west of the Mississippi with eight hundred miles of tracks extending from St. Louis in every direction. *Detail of Lloyd's Southern Railroad Map, 1863, Library of Congress*

RANAWAY,

From the residence of A. King, in St. Charles, on Wednesday night, the 2nd instant, my servant girl, named "ANN." She is a bright copper-colored mulatto, medium height, rather slight form, quite likely, and about 20 years of age.

Reward.

I will pay a reward of $25 for the arrest of said girl, if taken in St. Charles county, $50 if taken out of said county, and $100 if taken out of the State and returned to me or said King, in St. Charles

In 1857, the Supreme Court declared the Missouri Compromise unconstitutional in the celebrated Dred Scott case. Scott, a slave living in St. Louis, brought suit to gain his freedom. The controversial decision in this case was a boost to the proslavery faction and inflamed the anti-slavery adherents into militant action. *Library of Congress*

Slaves who ran away from their masters had avenues to freedom in the form of free states on Missouri's borders. Missouri slaveholders believed that the admission of Kansas as a free state would threaten the continued existence of slavery by surrounding Missouri on the east, north, and west by free states. *Missouri Historical Society, St. Louis*

for three decades. But the shaky compromise seemed to Thomas Jefferson to be a "firebell in the night." To Jefferson, "A geographical line, coinciding with a marked principle, moral and political, once conceived and held up to the angry passions of men, will never be obliterated; and every new irritation will mark it deeper and deeper." The Virginian, a slaveholder himself, was never more prophetic. Abolitionists and Southern "fire eaters" in the decades following the Missouri Compromise polarized the debate and increasingly eliminated any middle ground for mutual political accommodation.

By the late 1830s, there were Missouri laws that specified life imprisonment for abolitionist activities. During the same decade, Missourians drove Mormons from the state, in part due to their abolitionist tendencies. Missouri's United States senator, Thomas Hart Benton, a slaveholder, wrecked his political prominence when he deserted the slavery cause and favored the exclusion of slavery from former Mexican territories acquired as a result of the Mexican War (1846-1848). Immediately, the central clique of powerful Missouri slaveholders in the state legislature plotted Benton's downfall. Led by Claiborne Jackson, soon to become the pro-secession governor of Missouri, the clique orchestrated Old Bullion's defeat for reelection to the Senate, ending his illustrious thirty-year career as Missouri's senator.

Missouri was also at the epicenter of a Supreme Court decision handed down in 1857 that helped drive a final stake in the heart of the Missouri Compromise. The decision centered on a petition for freedom suit brought by a slave residing in St. Louis named Dred Scott. The case had begun in state courts eleven years earlier and finally ended up in the high court. As the property of an army surgeon, he had been taken first to Illinois and then to the Wisconsin Territory, both regions where slavery had been outlawed. Upon being returned to St. Louis, he brought suit against his owner on the claim that he was emancipated based on his residence in a free state and territory. The case drug on for years before Scott was finally declared free in a lower court. The aggrieved master immediately appealed the case to the Missouri Supreme Court, which now had a solid proslavery majority, and won. Scott then appealed to the nation's highest court where the case was accepted. In an intensely controversial declaration, the proslavery majority of the Supreme Court decreed in 1857 that Scott, as a black slave, was not a citizen and had no rights before the

PUBLIC MEETING!!

The Citizens of Batavia and Vicinity are requested to meet at ELLICOTT HALL, this (Monday) Evening at 7 o'clock, and hear an Address by the

Rev'd. Fred. Starr, Jr.

Who has been driven from his Post in Kansas as a Christian Missionary, (where he has resided with his Family for five years past,) at the Bidding and Dictation of the Slave Power.

Mr. STARR will Address the People on the Subject of the recent Outrages against the free Citizens of Kansas, by which the Right of Suffrage has been Invaded! The Pulpit Overthrown! The Missionaries Dispersed! The Press Destroyed! And the Liberty of Speech denied to Freemen.

Dated, Batavia, June 4th, 1855.

courts. In the process, the court declared the Missouri Compromise unconstitutional because Congress had no legal authority to forbid the taking of constitutionally protected private property (slaves) into the territories.

As it turned out, the Missouri Compromise was already moot by then. When Congress passed the Kansas-Nebraska Act of 1854, they repealed the compromise in favor of the doctrine of popular sovereignty. This act provided that the settlers of the Kansas and Nebraska territories would determine for themselves whether slavery would be allowed within their boundaries. Kansas, which was rapidly filling up with settlers, would be the first testing ground for popular sovereignty. The stakes in the outcome were high for both North and South; both sides believed the question of the future existence of slavery would be decided in the Kansas Territory. Because the Kansas Territory adjoined Missouri, Southerners believed they had the edge in making sure that Kansas entered the Union as a slave state. Indeed, the leaders of Missouri's Southern faction believed they could win Kansas for slavery. But Northern abolitionists were equally determined to keep Kansas free from the scourge of human bondage.

The stage was set for a confrontation that would give Missourians ("Pukes" or "Border Ruffians") and Kansans ("Jayhawkers") a five-year head start on the rest of the nation when it came to violence and bloodletting. As Missouri Senator David Rice Atchison put it in 1854: "We will … have the devil to pay in Kansas and this state. … We will be compelled to shoot, burn and hang, but the thing will soon be over. We intend to 'Mormonise' the Abolitionists." The other side was no less determined. Groups such as the New England Emigrant Aid Company provided both funds and arms to abolitionists who were willing to move to Kansas.

Missourians seemed to win the first round with a landslide victory in the election for members of the territorial legislature. On election day, March 30, 1855, gangs of Missourians, led by the likes of Atchison and Jackson, rode into Kansas and hijacked the state government by virtue of a fraudulent election in which there were 6,300 proslavery votes cast from an electorate of only 2,900 eligible voters. Such tactics ended up backfiring on the Missourians bent on using any means to gain

David Rice Atchison, a powerful senator and leader of the proslavery faction, took charge of the effort to ensure that Kansas would enter the Union as a slave state. In confronting Kansas Free-Soilers for control of the territory, he thundered, "We will be compelled to shoot, burn, and hang …" *Library of Congress*

Attempts by bands of Missouri "Border Ruffians," such as those who perhaps ran Reverend Fred Starr from his post in Kansas, to intimidate settlers and seize control of the territorial government by force and election fraud energized the Free State movement in northern states.
Used by permission, State Historical Society of Missouri, Columbia

control of Kansas affairs. The population of the Kansas Territory contained only a few New England abolitionists—4.3 percent of the total population. Most settlers in Kansas had come from the Midwest, and these migrants from the southern parts of Ohio, Indiana, and Illinois made up 22 percent of the population. This was a group that might have accepted slavery, but the election-grabbing tactics of Missourians made them feel like they had no voice in the territorial government that was being created at Lecompton. As a result they joined the ranks of the Free Staters in the struggle, not to prohibit slavery, but rather to control their own political destiny. Within months, a Free State government had been created at Topeka to oppose the Lecompton legislature set up by the bogus vote. This struggle soon moved from the ballot box into the arena of violence.

The result was an increasing number of border raids by both sides. The Bleeding Kansas period was inaugurated on May 21, 1856, when a gang of five hundred

In retaliation for an attack on Lawrence by a band of Missourians, the fanatical abolitionist John Brown and his sons murdered five pro-Southern settlers along Pottawatomie Creek. Events soon spiraled out of control, plunging Kansas into three years of bloody guerrilla warfare. *Library of Congress*

On May 19, 1858, a band of proslavery Missourians lined eleven Free Staters up in a ravine and fired, killing five of them. The Marais Des Cygnes Massacre became immortalized in a poem by John Greenleaf Whittier. *Kansas State Historical Society*

Border Ruffians surrounded the abolitionist stronghold of Lawrence and managed to burn down the Free State Hotel and smash the printing presses of two newspapers. Three days later, the fanatic John Brown and his sons retaliated by hacking five proslavery men to death with swords along Pottawatomie Creek.

For the next three years, guerrilla warfare raged along the Missouri-Kansas border. Bands of well-armed horsemen from both sides rode around the countryside driving off settlers, burning, looting, and plundering. In their wake were the ravaged landscapes that would be created on a far larger scale during the Civil War. By 1858, Jayhawker James Montgomery emerged as the scourge of proslavery men in southern Kansas and Missouri. He earned a reputation for acts of murder and for stealing the property and slaves of proslavery men along both sides of the border.

Montgomery's activities enraged Charles Hamilton and his band of Border

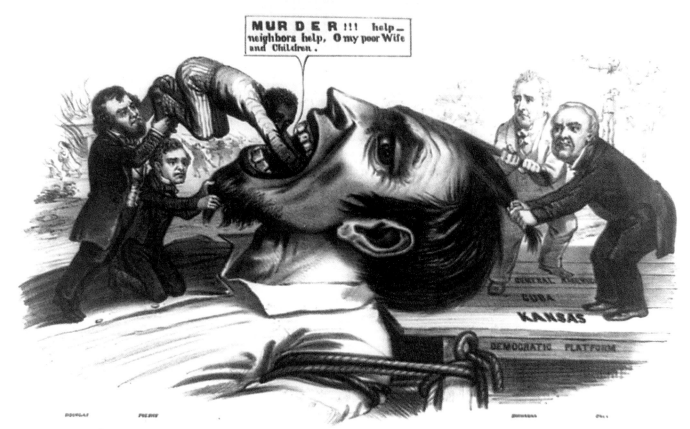

FORCING SLAVERY DOWN THE THROAT OF A FREESOILER

Ruffians. On May 19, 1858, Hamilton's men rounded up eleven Free Staters and lined them up in a ravine; Hamilton ordered his men to fire. Only five of the eleven were killed, and one man was missed entirely. This was the notorious "Marais Des Cygnes Massacre," immortalized by the New England poet John Greenleaf Whittier: "The foul human vultures/Have feasted and fled;/The Wolves of the Border/Have crept from the dead."

In December, John Brown and a group of horsemen crossed the border into Missouri and carried off eleven slaves. In true Jayhawker fashion, they also helped themselves to the horses, supplies, and property of their victims.

Estimates vary concerning how many people were killed during the Bleeding Kansas era. Numbers of deaths have ranged from as high as two hundred to as low as fifty-six. The number fifty-six was compiled by historian Dale Watts after a careful study of 157 violent deaths recorded during the territorial period. According to this count, proslavery forces bled the most with thirty lost, while twenty-four anti-slavery men fell; the persuasions of two other casualties are uncertain.

The struggle for Kansas was ultimately won by politics and demographics instead of violence. The Lecompton Constitution was voted on three times, and with election-stealing by Missourians removed from the equation, the constitution was rejected twice. In 1859, the Free State Wyandotte Constitution was drawn up and ratified by the voters by a two to one margin. Although the Kansas admission bill stalled in the pro-Southern Congress through 1860, President James Buchanan finally signed the bill to admit Kansas into the Union as a free state on January 29, 1861. By then Kansas had a population of 107,209. Only 13.5 percent of this

It was inevitable that the Free State cause would triumph simply because vastly more Northerners and Midwesterners made their homes in the plains of Kansas than did Southerners. Still, the entrance of Kansas into the Union as a free state was stymied by a pro-southern Congress until 1861. The cartoon depicts this faction shoving slavery down the throat of a Free-Soiler. *Library of Congress*

population came from states of the lower South. New Englanders constituted 16 percent, and the northern border states contributed 35 percent.

The stakes were high in the border war, but in the end, Missourians failed to influence Kansas. Ultimately, more Northerners and Midwesterners than Southerners were willing to make Kansas and its windswept plains home. One such Southerner, on his way back from a raid into Kansas during the bitterly cold winter of 1855-56, happened upon a woman living in a flimsy house sided with vertical planks. Bitterly cold winds whistled through the cracks in the boards. The woman huddled close to her sheet-iron stove, and tears streamed down her face. But these tears were not for her desperate situation. She was reading *Uncle Tom's Cabin* and wept for the plight of slaves. In the raider's estimation, the slaves this woman wept for were far more comfortable and well off in their warm quarters than was this lady abolitionist struggling to survive on the freezing, inhospitable plains of Kansas.

Southerners, in the end, found Kansas to be unlikable land. They were loath to leave behind the familiar rolling, forested landscapes of Missouri and elsewhere in the South—the kind of terrain they had dwelled on for generations as they spread as far as western Missouri before they reached the edge of the great Eastern Woodlands. Beyond the forests, they encountered an alien and unfamiliar landscape. The endless prairies stretching westward as far as the eye could see were a barrier to advancement of Southern culture that was formed by nature, not politics.

The next great struggle for the people of Missouri was forced upon the state by outside forces—the election of Abraham Lincoln and the consequent secession of the states of the Deep South. As 1861 dawned, Missourians would have to sort out the internal contradictions of a state that was in every sense a border state torn in two opposing directions. It was a potentially deadly situation. As the great Civil War historian Bruce Catton once observed:

"Here was a state still close to the frontier, where men were predisposed to violence and where half a decade of dispute over the slavery issue had created many enmities, the lines of hatred running from farm to farm and from neighbor to neighbor. Altogether, it was a bad state in which to ignite a civil war."

1861

VOTERS NEEDED SCORE cards to keep up with all the twists and turns of the election of 1860 that put Abraham Lincoln, an Illinois lawyer with relatively little office-holding experience, into the White House. By the time this election had rolled around, the political landscape of the nation had changed profoundly. The slavery question was the cause. The Democrats were split into Northern and Southern factions. The Whig party had also divided into "conscience Whigs" versus "cotton Whigs." Even the American, or "Know Nothing," party, founded in the 1840s to resist the tide of foreign immigration from Ireland and Germany—mainly Catholics descending upon a Protestant nation—and named for its semi-secret beginnings, had parted company over slavery. The Kansas-Nebraska Act had brought the issue of the extension of slavery to the front burner and served as a catalyst for the creation of the Republican Party. With Southerners becoming more strident and insistent on the protection of slavery, the Republicans offered a new political home for disenchanted Whigs, Democrats, and Know Nothings who were opposed to the spread of slavery into the western territories.

The front-runner for the Democratic Party presidential nomination was from

Abraham Lincoln, as photographed by Matthew Brady in February of 1860. As president, Lincoln was keenly aware of the importance of keeping Missouri in the Union. *Library of Congress, Reenactment list, Steve Wilson*

From left: Senator Stephen Douglas may have been defeated by his fellow Illinoian, Abraham Lincoln, in the presidential race, but in Missouri, he defeated Lincoln soundly and edged out the Constitutional Unionist to carry Missouri. John C. Breckinridge of Kentucky headed the Southern Democratic ticket for president. Breckinridge fared poorly with the voters, garnering only enough votes to place third. John Bell of Tennessee, who garnered a close second, represented the Constitutional Union party. The party's slavery-with-Union stance appealed to Missouri voters. *Library of Congress*

11

Jefferson Davis of Mississippi, as president of the Confederate States of America, got off to a bad start with Missouri's secessionist leaders. The seemingly contradictory actions of Gov. Claiborne Jackson and Maj. Gen. Sterling Price during the early months of the secession crisis convinced him that the two leaders were negotiating simultaneously with the Confederate and Union governments and could not, therefore, be trusted. The result was that Missouri's relations with the Confederacy were badly damaged at the very moment when the state's struggling secessionist movemnt needed all the help it could get. *Library of Congress*

The United States in 1861, as shown on a military map of the states and territories printed by P. S. Duval & Son, Philadelphia. Red indicates border states, blue indicates a seceding state, orange is a free state, and green is a new state. *Library of Congress*

MILITARY MAP
OF THE
UNITED STATES & TERRITORIES
Showing
The Location of the Military Posts, Arsenals
Navy Yards, & Ports of Entry
Compiled from Pub. Dec. 1861.
Published by P.S. Duval & Son,

Lincoln's state, Illinois, and defeated the Rail-Splitter for a seat in the Senate in 1858. He was Senator Stephen Douglas, the celebrated proponent of popular sovereignty. He tried to carve out a middle ground between the quarreling factions of his party, but in the end ended up satisfying neither. His proposal to allow each new state to determine for itself whether to enter the Union as a slave or free state was unacceptable to most Southerners and many Northerners.

Southern Democrats insisted that slavery could not be restricted from any state or territory—a conviction confirmed by the Supreme Court in the Dred Scott decision of 1857—and bolted from the party loyal to Douglas. They nominated their own candidate, John Breckinridge of Kentucky, to run against both Douglas and Lincoln, who had become the Republican Party candidate and an avowed Free-Soiler. To complete the confusion, die-hard members of the old Whig and Know Nothing parties refashioned themselves as the Constitutional Union Party (slavery with Union) and fielded John Bell of Tennessee as their candidate.

With the Democratic Party split and the Constitutional Unionists drawing still other votes away from the Douglas Democrats, Lincoln gained the victory. Even though he polled only 40 percent of the national votes cast in this four-way race, it was enough to give him the 180 electoral votes needed to win the presidency. In the North, however, Lincoln garnered a solid six of ten votes cast; Breckinridge, in turn, carried all of the Deep South. Lincoln's victory proved to Southern fire-eaters that the prophecy of Senator John C. Calhoun of South Carolina had come to pass, "The great and primary cause [of danger] is that the equilibrium between the two sections has been destroyed."

Less than two months after Lincoln's election, South Carolina became the first state to secede from the Union. By the beginning of February 1861, six more states—Mississippi, Florida, Alabama, Georgia, Louisiana, and Texas—followed suit. Delegates from those states gathered in Montgomery, Alabama, to draft a constitution creating the Confederate States of America. They also selected Jefferson Davis as the first and only president of the Confederacy. His résumé as West Point

graduate, Mexican War veteran, planter, United States congressman and senator from Mississippi, and Secretary of War was far more impressive than that of the upstart Illinois attorney who was the newly elected president of the United States.

But Jefferson Davis's Confederacy was vulnerable in many ways. It claimed only 10 percent of the nation's white population and 5 percent of its industrial establishment. And not all slave states had come aboard. Yet to declare were the eight states of the upper and border South: Delaware, Maryland, Virginia, North Carolina, Tennessee, Kentucky, Arkansas, and Missouri. The stakes were high for winning the allegiance of these states, which accounted for more than half of the population of the South and produced half of the region's horses and mules, three-fifths of its livestock and cereal crops, and three-quarters of its industrial capability.

Of the undecided states, Missouri was an especially choice plum for the picking. The most populous state west of the Mississippi River, Missouri ranked third nationally in corn and pork production and ranked high as a producer of grain and livestock. Missouri horses and mules were known throughout the country. Mineral districts in the southern part of the state contained rich deposits of iron and lead, and Missouri's manufacturing establishments produced a wide variety of products that would be useful to a war effort. They included James B. Eads's boatyard at Carondelet near St. Louis, a facility where the river man would soon build the ironclad gunboats used by Generals John Pope and Ulysses Grant to open the Mississippi and Tennessee rivers. Also radiating from St. Louis were several railroads penetrating the state's interior in every direction.

All of these factors added up to Missouri possessing vital strategic importance as a breadbasket and supply depot for the nation that possessed its borders and many resources. Its location made it the northwest flank of the Trans-Mississippi theater in the coming war. There was no predestined logic to disunion; whoever controlled Missouri gained an important advantage. It represented a potential Southern dagger poised at the Union heartland. Conversely, Union control of the state through the urban hub at St. Louis would give it mastery of the Missouri River as well as a significant stretch of the Mississippi, an avenue bisecting the lower South all the way to the Gulf of Mexico.

This bird's-eye view looking south at the junction of the Mississippi and Ohio rivers at the time of the Civil War depicts the stretches of the Mississippi to be fought over as each side attempted to control this vital artery of commerce and transportation. The Confederate fortifications at Columbus, Kentucky; New Madrid, Missouri; and Island No. 10 were to fall within the crosshairs of Ulysses S. Grant and John Pope in late 1861 and early 1862. *Library of Congress*

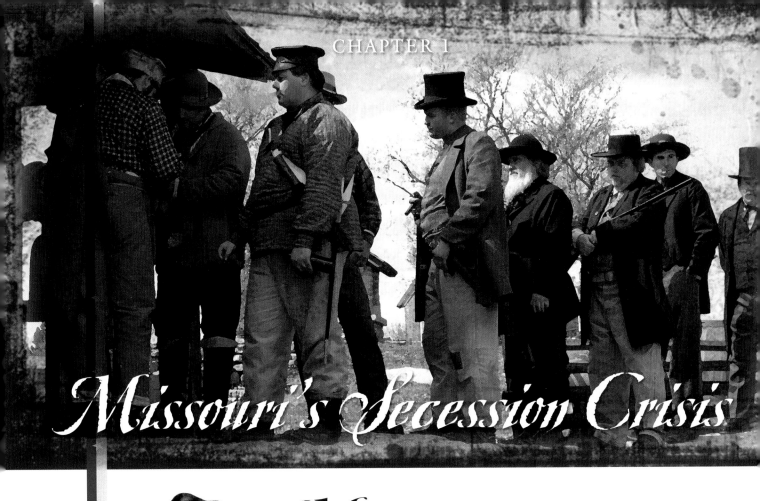

CHAPTER 1

Missouri's Secession Crisis

MISSOURIANS IN THE election of 1860 gave no clear indication of the direction the state would take as the political crisis worsened. On the surface it appeared that moderates had won. Republicans received scant votes in the statewide election. Most Republican support came from St. Louis German Americans. Likewise, the southern-sympathizing Breckinridge faction fared little better with most of its support coming not from the plantation districts along the Missouri River but from the Ozarks. In the races for governor and lieutenant governor, the Douglas Democrats, who supported self-determination, and Constitutional Unionists, who supported the Union with slavery, divided the vote with a plurality going to Claiborne Fox Jackson and Thomas C. Reynolds, the Douglas candidates. Their election confused the situation because Jackson and Reynolds were avowed secessionists and Breckinridge loyalists, but they had embraced Douglas and his party in the name of political expediency.

If heartfelt convictions could be gauged, secessionist candidates probably garnered a majority of votes cast. But voters hardly gave

Claiborne Fox Jackson became governor in 1860. Although he ran as a Douglas Democrat, he was at heart a secessionist. *John M. McElroy, "The Struggle for Missouri"*

Reenactment photo(top), Steve Wilson

Thomas C. Reynolds was born in South Carolina, educated in Virginia, and arrived in Missouri in 1850. He was elected Lieutenant Governor in 1860. *Governor's Portrait Gallery, Missouri State Capitol*

Jackson and Reynolds a secessionist mandate. Moderates from the Douglas and Constitutional Union factions comprised the majority in both legislative houses of the Twenty-First General Assembly, but there were strong Breckinridge minorities as well: 15 of 33 seats in the Senate, and 47 of 133 House seats.

Once elected, Jackson was not long in casting off his Douglas sheep's clothing and revealing his true stance, though he was not yet ready to officially announce his commitment to a secessionist course. In his inaugural address on January 3, 1861, he boldly proclaimed: "The destiny of the slaveholding states of this union is one and the same. So long as a state maintains slavery within her limits, it is impossible to separate her fate from that of her sister states. ... Missouri will not be found to shrink from the duty, which her position on the border imposes; her honor, her interests, and her sympathies point alike in one direction, and determine her *to stand by the South.*"

Having uttered those fighting words, Jackson and the leading secessionists began planning to take the state down that path. First, Jackson needed to call a convention along the lines of those held in all the seceding states. He hoped it would produce the same result, a vote for secession. Then he needed to raise a state army to take on any Federal forces sent by Lincoln to enforce loyalty. To accomplish this end, he hoped to persuade the General Assembly to pass a military bill granting him sweeping authority to compel military service from every military-aged male in the state. Finally, Jackson coveted the store of military weapons and equipment in the United States Arsenal at St. Louis and hoped to place them in the hands of the scores of volunteers he expected to flock to the standard of the South. These were the high stakes in the great game that was to be played out in the next few months. To the winner would go possession of the city of St. Louis and its great arsenal, military dominance of the state, and most likely, the destiny of Missouri.

Jackson immediately ran into trouble getting his military bill passed. Conservative

By the dawn of the Civil War, the United States Arsenal at St. Louis, established in 1827, contained a store of thirty thousand muskets, ninety thousand pounds of powder, and forty field pieces—enough weaponry to outfit an entire army to fight under Gov. Claiborne Jackson for the South. But first Jackson had to devise a plan to seize the arsenal. *Postcard drawing, John Bradbury Collection*

15

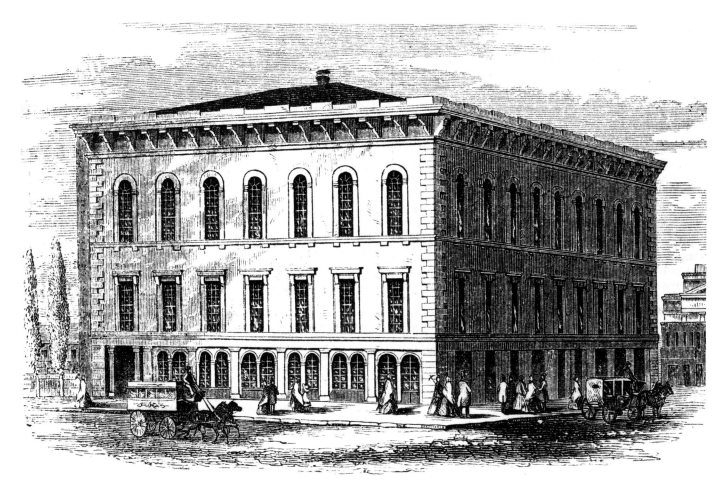

During March of 1861, the elegant St. Louis Mercantile Library, built in 1854 at the corner of Fifth and Pine streets, was the location of a State Convention authorized by the General Assembly to "consider the relations of the State of Missouri to the United States." This convention disappointed secessionist leaders, such as Gov. Claiborne Jackson, by declaring that there was "at present no adequate cause to impel Missouri to dissolve her connection with the federal Union." *Used by permission, State Historical Society of Missouri, Columbia*

members of the General Assembly were not yet willing to adopt such a sweeping measure but, over the objections of Unionists, overwhelmingly authorized a convention to "consider the relations of the State of Missouri to the United States." If they had believed the convention would stand with the seceded states, Jackson and secessionist leaders, all seasoned politicians, had made a grave misjudgment based on the results of the vote for convention delegates. All the delegates elected to the convention were either Conditional or Unconditional Unionists. As long as the Conditional Unionists, who favored Missouri retaining its unionist ties so long as slavery was protected and the seceding Southern states were not coerced by the North, and the Unconditional Unionists, who demanded no conditions, could unify on the position that Missouri should remain in the Union, they controlled Missouri's destiny. Not a single secessionist candidate was elected.

Most of the convention's business was conducted in the St. Louis Mercantile Library during the month of March 1861. Former governor Sterling Price presided and Judge Hamilton Gamble chaired the Committee on Federal Relations. Predictably, the convention delegates found that while the state remained attached to its Southern institutions (notably, slavery) and its delegates hoped that they could reach a compromise with the seceded states, there was "at present no adequate cause to impel Missouri to dissolve her connection with the federal Union."

The calling of a convention unwilling to secede was a serious setback to Jackson's agenda. Now that his perceived mandate had evaporated, Jackson the ardent secessionist was hamstrung by Jackson the parliamentarian. He did not have the ruthless temperament to stage a coup d'état and seize control of government. He required an adequate cause, procedural or otherwise, to act. At a time when the secession cause desperately needed aggressive maneuvers, Jackson became mired in the contentiousness of Missouri politics. M. Jeff Thompson, former mayor of St. Joseph and ardent secessionist who would shortly be stirring things up in southeast Missouri, stormed into Jackson's office around this time and bellowed: "Governor, before I leave, I wish to tell you the two qualities of a soldier. One he must have, but he needs both. One of them is common sense, and the other is courage—and by God! You have *neither*."

Jackson's chief rival and threat in the struggle to take Missouri out of the Union was Francis Preston "Frank" Blair, Jr. A scion of one of America's most distinguished political families, Blair was as determined to keep Missouri in the Union as Jackson was to take her out. However, Frank was an outsider, not a part of the Jefferson City political clique. His seat in the United States House of Representatives derived from his base among the German-American voters in St. Louis. As such, he was unencumbered in his actions by the lack of approval from the Southern-leaning politicians who controlled Missouri's state government. Frank Blair was also a personal friend of the president, and his brother, Montgomery Blair, was Lincoln's postmaster general. Through his brother, he had the president's ear, and Lincoln employed Frank as his manager of events in Missouri during the crucial early months of 1861. Blair was a decisive man who worked smart—smarter than his powerful and entrenched foes. An adversary, Thomas Snead, said this of him, "[Blair] went on busily organizing and consolidating his forces, preparing systematically, earnestly, and intelligently for war, and doing everything that a statesman and soldier could do to hold Missouri loyal to the Union, which he believed to be the source of all her prosperity."

Francis Preston Blair, Jr. came from one of America's most distinguished political families. He was determined to keep Missouri in the Union. *John M. McElroy, "The Struggle for Missouri"*

In addition to direct access to Lincoln, Frank Blair mustered in these early months a larger and better trained military force than did Jackson, even though he had no statewide following. His weapon for going toe-to-toe with secessionists was the large contingent of German Americans in St. Louis. They were already organized into Turnverein or Turner clubs, social organizations that could easily be converted to political or military purposes. While the supporters of Claiborne Jackson and Thomas Reynolds organized a diverse force of young Southern gentlemen and Dutch-hating Irish immigrants of St. Louis into paramilitary bands called Minute Men, Blair vigorously organized his Germans into Wide Awake political clubs, shortly to be transformed into Home Guard military units for federal service. The Minute Men tauntingly flew a Confederate flag from their headquarters in the Berthold Mansion and hatched plans to seize the St. Louis Arsenal. At the same time, Blair's Wide Awakes drilled secretly at night, preparing for armed confrontation. It seemed that extremists, not moderates, would determine the course of events in Missouri.

Blair was greatly aided by the arrival, on February 6, 1861, of a fiery Regular Army (the permanent military force of the United States, versus volunteers raised during wartime) captain named Nathaniel Lyon. A hot-tempered New Englander and West Pointer, Lyon was also a passionate abolitionist who held slaveholding and slaveholders in complete contempt after experiencing Kansas during the border troubles. And he had a steely determination to match Blair's. William Tecumseh Sherman, who saw Lyon in St. Louis during this time, described this energetic and frenetic officer, "his hair in the wind ... wild and irregular ... a man of vehement purpose and of determined action." Blair and Lyon were to prove an unbeatable team.

Nathaniel Lyon allied with Frank Blair to form an unbeatable team. *John M. McElroy, "The Struggle for Missouri"*

Had Jackson acted immediately after his January inauguration, he might have

The Bartholomew Berthold Mansion served as the gathering place for a force of young Southern gentlemen and Dutch-hating Irish immigrants of St. Louis who styled themselves Minute Men and tauntingly flew the Confederate flag above their headquarters. *John Albury Bryan, "Missouri's Contribution to American Architecture," St. Louis Architectural Club, 1928*

stood a fair chance of seizing the St. Louis Arsenal. His agent in St. Louis, Gen. Daniel Marsh Frost, reported that he had visited the commander of the arsenal, Maj. William H. Bell, who confided, "He had arms for forty thousand men, with the appliances to manufacture munitions of almost every kind." Bell, a native of the South and a secessionist sympathizer, was willing to turn over control of the arsenal and its stores to state authorities.

"I found the Major everything that you or I could desire," Frost concluded. Jackson decided to postpone any seizure until the state convention met, as he expected an ordinance of secession, but he waited too long. Blair and Lyon, aware of Jackson's machinations, watched his every move and prepared countermoves of their own.

The firing on Fort Sumter, April 12, 1861, gave Jackson another opportunity to grasp the "adequate cause" required by still-wavering moderates in the state legislature. The incident galvanized Virginia, North Carolina, Tennessee, and Arkansas to secede, but despite all the excitement, the General Assembly was still not ready to bolt the Union. However, the governor threw down a gauntlet, responding on April 17 to Lincoln's call for the states to furnish troops with the thunderous statement: "Your requisition, in my judgment, is illegal, unconstitutional, and revolutionary in its objects, inhuman and diabolical, and cannot be complied with. Not one man will the state of Missouri furnish to carry on such an unholy crusade."

This defiant bellicosity backfired on Jackson. The General Assembly still refused to pass Jackson's military bill, but the governor's fiery pronouncement got Lincoln's attention. Frank Blair contacted Lincoln to inform him that if Jackson would not provide the called-for troops, he could. Lincoln immediately authorized Blair to enlist and arm 10,000 troops. Within two weeks, Lyon signed up 2,500 men, 80 percent of them German Americans. Several thousand more enlisted in the weeks that followed.

Missouri's secessionist forces did manage to seize a Federal arsenal—tiny Liberty Arsenal in Clay County. Here, a group of local Southern men made off with 1,500 rifles and muskets, several cannons, and a large supply of powder and ammunition on April 20. They would soon put the arms to good use, but the haul hardly compensated for the vastly larger trove of weapons in St. Louis. This far vaster stock had remained at the lightly defended arsenal through the entire month of January, almost begging to be seized. But the Liberty Arsenal seizure and rumors that secessionists intended to storm the arsenal motivated Lyon on April 24 to have the

Two hundred pro-Southern horsemen seized the Federal Arsenal at Liberty just ten days after the first shots were fired on Fort Sumter. The haul from this facility hardly matched the trove of weapons at the St. Louis arsenal but still yielded a modest amount of badly needed weapons for the Southerners.
Century Magazine, May 1887

Gen. Daniel Marsh Frost commanded the First Brigade of the Missouri State Militia, encamped at Camp Jackson when it was surrounded by a force of 6,000 men commanded by Frank Blair and Nathaniel Lyon. Frost surrendered himself and 690 men with an indignant protest that his encampment was legal. Blair and Lyon also knew he was actively conspiring to capture the St. Louis Arsenal and had received siege guns from Jefferson Davis for that purpose. *Missouri Historical Society, St. Louis*

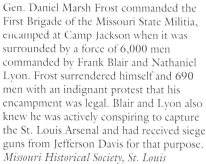

Lindell's Grove, now covered by the Frost Campus at St. Louis University, was the site of Camp Jackson. This is a rare image of the encampment of the First Brigade of the Missouri Militia, which was an eleven-day muster that commenced on May 6, 1861, and ended in capture by forces commanded by Nathaniel Lyon and Frank Blair. *Missouri Historical Society, St. Louis*

bulk of the arms and munitions transferred from the armory across the Mississippi to Illinois. While he removed the weapons from the reach of the secessionists, he wisely held back enough muskets to arm his new volunteers.

The secessionists, as it turned out, never knew the object of their desire had slipped their grasp. At the same time he fired off his defiant response to Lincoln, Jackson made his first official contacts with the Confederacy, sending representatives to Jefferson Davis asking for siege guns to reduce the stout, well-defended stone walls of the St. Louis Arsenal. Davis complied by sending Jackson two twelve-pounder fieldpieces and two thirty-two-pounder guns recently seized from the U.S. Arsenal at Baton Rouge, Louisiana. He also expressed the hope that the star of Missouri would soon be added to the constellation of Confederate states. Jackson then ordered the annual encampment of the Missouri militia to take place in St. Louis. Originally the state encampment was to be located on the heights above the arsenal, but Lyon alertly occupied the high ground with his own troops. State militiamen under Gen. Daniel M. Frost thereupon set up Camp Jackson at Lindell's Grove on the western outskirts of the city.

These actions led to the next to last incident that tilted Missouri toward secession—the Camp Jackson Affair. It was a tragic event that probably didn't need to happen. Governor Jackson and General Frost intended to seize the arsenal with a military force at some point, but by the time the First Brigade of the Missouri State Militia and a contingent of Minute Men, comprising 891 men, had set up camp on May 6, 1861, there was nothing left in the arsenal to seize and a large well-armed federal force of perhaps 8,000 men to contend with if they tried. At the

The Camp Jackson Massacre occurred when an angry pro-Southern crowd clashed with freshly enlisted German-American soldiers after the capture of Camp Jackson. The end result, twenty-eight civilians killed by soldiers, inflamed Southern sentiment in the state and led to the creation of the pro-Southern Missouri State Guard. Four federal soldiers and three captive militiamen also died. *Missouri Historical Society, St. Louis*

Gen. William S. Harney commanded military forces at St. Louis during the tense early months of 1861. Lyon and Blair suspected Harney was soft on secessionism, because he had married into a prominent and wealthy St. Louis Southern family, and wanted him recalled from duty. His demise was hastened by the ill-advised Price-Harney Agreement of May 21, 1861. *Missouri Historical Society, St. Louis*

same time, the militia members blatantly displayed their Southern proclivities by naming the camp's streets in honor of prominent secessionists Jefferson Davis and Pierre G. T. Beauregard. They also received the artillery weapons sent by Jefferson Davis, which arrived at the St. Louis riverfront in large crates marked "Tamaroa marble" and were hauled by wagon to Camp Jackson. Lyon and Blair knew all this, supposedly due to Lyon's scout of the camp while disguised as an elderly matron in a bombazine dress, his flowing red beard concealed behind a veil.

Had Blair and Lyon been moderate men, they might have concluded that the forces at Camp Jackson offered no threat to the arsenal and that they could simply be allowed go through the motions of their eleven-day muster before returning peacefully to their homes. But such a pacific and accommodating course of action was simply not in the makeup of either Lyon or Blair. Camp Jackson represented their best opportunity to stamp out blatant and defiant secessionism in the city, capture the largest organized military force the secessionists had, and bring St. Louis under Federal control.

The ranking U. S. military official in St. Louis was Gen. William Harney. He was a distinguished veteran of long years in Federal service and a moderate in temperament and action, but he was also an in-law of the wealthy Mullanphy family, leading St. Louis secessionists. Blair and Lyon felt that Harney was too moderate to deal with the urgent threat posed by crafty and determined secessionists actively plotting against the federal government. They had managed through Montgomery Blair to have Harney called to Washington for consultations on Missouri, leaving Lyon in temporary command. But Harney was on his way back to St. Louis; they had to act immediately.

If they seized Camp Jackson by force, Blair and Lyon knew they ran the risk of handing Claiborne Jackson the incident he needed to tilt the fragile loyalty of Conditional Unionists, thereby shocking the General Assembly into giving the governor all the military power he sought. But they were high-stakes gamblers. In the early afternoon of May 10, only a day before the state encampment was to disband, Lyon and Blair marched at the head of 6,000 armed soldiers, mainly German Americans, in the direction of Camp Jackson.

General Frost learned that a large Federal force was heading toward the state militia camp. He sent Lyon an indignant message protesting that his force was participating in a legal muster of the state militia. That was true, but General Frost had also actively participated in a conspiracy to seize a federal arsenal, which definitely wasn't legal. He had time enough to organize a defense of Camp Jackson, march his men away to fight another day, or even furlough his men so that they could dissolve into the city and surrounding countryside. But Frost took the most perplexing and unexplainable option available to him—he simply did nothing but wait with his men to be captured by Lyon and Blair. By mid-afternoon, the Union forces arrived at Lindell's Grove, surrounded the camp, and sent a demand for unconditional surrender. Frost had no choice but to accept. Lyon captured 690 officers and men along with their arms; federal marshals also replevined the Baton Rouge siege guns.

After a long delay organizing the prisoners for the march back to the arsenal, the most tragic phase of the Camp Jackson Affair began. By the time Lyon's force began their return march, a large crowd filled with Southern sympathizers lined the streets. First epithets, then brickbats, were hurled at the "damned Dutch."

Shots rang out from the crowd, killed Capt. Constantin Blandowski and three other soldiers, and wounded several more. Three captive state militiamen were also hit. Inexperienced and frightened, Federal soldiers began, without orders, firing volleys into the crowd, which was mostly composed of innocent spectators. The spectators stampeded in panic. Twenty-eight were left dead, including a twelve-year-old boy and a fourteen-year-old girl. Many more were wounded.

The next day, in downtown St. Louis, there was another clash between a large angry mob and a troop of 1,000 raw German-American soldiers. As on the previous day, the crowd started with jeers, then began throwing stones. Shots from the crowd dropped four soldiers with fatal wounds before the troops responded again by shooting wildly into the crowd. This time, nine civilians ended up dead.

Bruce Catton summed up the hornet's nest that had been so violently shaken: "Blair and Lyon had won the civil war in St. Louis before it really got started, which was just what they set out to do, but as far as the rest of the state was concerned, they had won nothing; they had simply made more civil war inevitable. The fighting in St. Louis was clear warning that the middle of the road was no path for Missourians. No longer would carefree militiamen lounge picturesquely in a picnic-ground camp, serenading the girls while they waited for glory and an easy triumph. Now they would fight, and other men would fight against them, and no part of the United States would know greater bitterness or misery." Camp Jackson provided the first instance of zealous or overzealous Federal harshness toward Missourians. It was a long way from being the last.

Camp Jackson struck Missourians like a thunderbolt. Finally, Jackson had the opportunity he had been seeking, and the General Assembly waffled no more.

The day following the capture of Camp Jackson, May 11, 1861, a pro-Southern mob clashed with raw German-American enlistees in the streets of St. Louis. Nine civilians and four soldiers ended up dead. *Harper's Weekly*

Reports started coming in from all corners of the state that secessionists were boldly asserting themselves with impunity. Mobs hauled down and burned United States flags and confiscated stores of powder and lead. Confederate troops were reportedly already gathering in southwest Missouri, and organization of State Guard units moved forward at a rapid pace.

Amidst rumors that Lyon and Blair and their Teutonic minions were already en route to Jefferson City, the legislators met in an extraordinary all-night session. At last, Governor Jackson got his military bill, and with it, the absolute powers he had long sought to create and equip a state guard capable of resisting Federal invasion. Lukewarm Unionists now flocked to the Southern camp in large numbers, rapidly filling the nascent State Guard with eager volunteers. Sterling Price, the popular former governor, Mexican War hero, and reluctant secessionist, now offered his considerable military experience to the Southern cause. Jackson had profound doubts about Price—he had recently served as president of the "submission" convention that voted to keep Missouri in the Union—but Lieutenant Governor Reynolds persuaded Jackson that Price would be a valuable addition to the cause. Jackson commissioned Price as a major general and placed him in charge of the Missouri State Guard. Both men would soon have cause to regret this decision.

At this juncture, Jackson and Reynolds now had the legal authorization they wanted to create a state military force, but they needed time to organize and train this force. It was time that Blair and Lyon might not allow them. And there was the matter of how to secede from the Union. At this point, Jackson and Reynolds wanted to reconvene the state convention, but they were well aware that Lyon and Blair would not stand by idly while a convention drew up an ordinance of secession. Jackson stated his dilemma to a correspondent in St. Louis: "I do not think Missouri should secede today or tomorrow, but I do not think I should *publicly so declare*, I want a little time to arm the state, and I am assuming every responsibility to do it with all possible dispatch. [Missouri] should have gone out last winter when she could have seized public arms and public property and defended herself. This she has failed to do and must now wait a little while."

About this time Jackson and Reynolds began to work at cross purposes with each other. Jackson had determined, without consulting Reynolds, to send an emissary to Jefferson Davis requesting that Confederate troops enter Missouri to protect the convention while it carried out the business of secession. Reynolds also determined to go to Davis with the same plea but different motives. Unbeknownst to Jackson, Reynolds met with Price and shared with him his concern that Jackson was too given to temporizing and might even succumb to a policy of neutrality, which could be fatal to the cause of secession. Price agreed and stated that he, as president of the convention, was willing to give Reynolds written authority to go to Davis and seek the protection of the Confederate army.

Reynolds was vaguely aware that Jackson had asked Price to meet with General Harney, who had returned to St. Louis and resumed command of the Department of the West. The governor hoped to achieve some kind of temporary neutrality, averting a confrontation between state and federal forces long enough to give him and Price time to carry out their plans for secession. The result of the meeting was the Price-Harney Agreement. It turned out to be an unmitigated disaster that ended Harney's career as well as caused irreparable damage to Jackson's hopes for cooperating with Jefferson Davis's Confederacy.

Harney and Price met in St. Louis on May 21 and drafted their infamous agreement. Price, as commander of the State Guard, pledged to use the whole power of the state to respect the rights of all persons, suppress all unlawful proceedings, and maintain order within the state. Ever cautious and moderate, the Federal commander bargained with Price in good faith, hoping to calm the public passions inflamed by the recent events. He agreed that as long as order prevailed, no Federal military movements would be made into the state. Harney then published a proclamation that stated "that the united forces of both Governments are pledged to the maintenance of the peace of the State, and the defense of the rights and property of all persons, without distinction of party. This pledge ... will be by both [federal and state authorities] most religiously and sacredly kept, and, if necessary to put down evil-disposed persons, the military powers of both Governments will be called out to enforce the terms of the honorable and amicable agreement which has been made."

Jefferson Davis heard of the Price-Harney Agreement about the same time he received requests from Jackson's emissary, Edward Cabell, and from Lieutenant Governor Reynolds to send Confederate troops into Missouri. Davis, a Southerner with a high sense of honor and propriety, immediately developed a profound distrust of Jackson, who had blessed the agreement Price had made. How could he trust a governor who was requesting soldiers from a foreign government to invade Missouri and protect his state against incursions by the federal government, while at the same time pledging to the same federal government that he would cooperate with them to resist any foreign invasion? Davis wanted to have nothing to do with men who talked out of both sides of their mouths. Missouri's relations with the Confederacy were badly damaged at the very moment when the state's struggling secessionist movement needed all the help it could get.

Blair and Lyon believed Harney to be naive and weak and were incensed by his agreement with Price. Fired by the urgency of the situation, they viewed with alarm the speed with which their foes moved to control large areas of out-state Missouri. Southern organizers were hard at work everywhere, recruiting and preparing to train an army to oppose the federal government's authority. Lyon champed at the bit to drive the secessionists out of their lair at the state capital, occupy the major towns along the Missouri River and the railheads, and drive a wedge between Gen. Ben McCulloch's Confederate troops in northwest Arkansas and any army Price might try to send that way. On the heels of the Price-Harney Agreement, reports started coming in from all corners of the state that secessionists were boldly asserting themselves with impunity. Mobs hauled down and burned United States flags and confiscated stores of powder and lead. Confederate troops were reportedly already gathering in southwest Missouri, and organization of State Guard units moved forward at a rapid pace. Union citizens throughout the state complained of harassment and threats by their Southern neighbors.

On June 10, 1861, Claiborne
Jackson and Gen. Sterling
Price met with Frank Blair
and Gen. Nathaniel Lyon
at the Planter's House in
St. Louis. Jackson and Price
urged a neutrality treaty
between federal and state
armies, but Lyon angrily
rejected this, saying that he
would rather see every man,
woman, and child in the
state dead and buried before
conceding federal authority
to the state. He ended the
fateful meeting with the terse
statement: "This means war.
In an hour one of my officers
will call for you and conduct
you out of my lines."
*John M. McElroy, "The
Struggle for Missouri"*

Although Lincoln urged him to use discretion and restraint before revealing it, Blair soon had in his pocket the president's order removing Harney from command and appointing Lyon in his place. It was a courageous decision on Lincoln's part because General Harney had many influential Republican supporters in St. Louis. However, Lyon and Blair refused to stand by and give their enemies free rein. By May 30, they concluded that Harney had to go. Blair delivered Lincoln's order relieving the venerable old soldier, and Lyon assumed command.

Jackson and Price, still desperate to buy more time, hoped to stall Lyon and Blair awhile longer. But this required a face-to-face parley with two of the most adamant and distrusting political antagonists they could ever meet. Arrangements were made for the epic confrontation in St. Louis.

The fateful meeting at the Planter's House Hotel in St. Louis took place on June 10, 1861. Lyon and Blair and aide-de-camp Maj. Horace Conant sat opposite Jackson, Price, and Thomas Snead, Price's aide-de-camp. Jackson proposed a neutrality treaty, as if he were negotiating with a foreign nation, under which the State Guard and the Unionist Home Guard units would disarm and state authorities would suppress all insurrectionary activities outside of St. Louis. Blair was supposed to handle the Unionist side of the discussion, but Lyon entered the exchange and soon dominated the negotiations. Snead described Lyon's forceful performance at this extraordinary meeting: "In half an hour it was [Lyon] that was conducting [the meeting], holding his own at every point against Jackson and Price, masters though they were of Missouri politics whose course they had been directing and controlling for years while he was only captain of an infantry regiment on the Plains."

The meeting dragged on for four or five hours before Lyon finally had enough of fruitless discussion and rose to conclude the interview. His words, as set down by Snead, struck like lightening: "Rather than concede to the state of Missouri the right to demand that my government shall not enlist troops within her limits, or bring troops into the state whenever it pleases, or move its troops at its own will into, out of, or through the state; rather than to concede to the state of Missouri for one single instant the right to dictate to my government in any matter however unimportant, I would *(rising as he said this, and pointing in turn to everyone in the room)* see you, and you, and you, and you, and you, and every man, woman, and child in the state dead and buried. *(Then turning to Governor Jackson)* This means war. In an hour one of my officers will call for you and conduct you out of my lines."

Jackson, Price, and Snead did not wait for Lyon's escort but departed immediately for Jefferson City. Along with every other Missourian, they hurtled into uncharted and frightening territory in which the rules for survival had not yet been written.

CHAPTER 2

The Road to Boonville

Before retreating from the capital with his now fugitive government, Gov. Claiborne F. Jackson called for 50,000 volunteers to step forward to resist federal aggression. By mid-June only 1,500 enlistees had reported to Camp Bacon, east of Boonville. Before they could be drilled or armed, Gen. Nathaniel Lyon launched his attack. The Battle of Boonville was fought on June 17, 1861, five weeks before Bull Run. *Reenactment photo, Jim Smith*

*A*FTER THE MEETING at the Planter's House broke up, Price, Jackson, and Snead hurried immediately to the Pacific Railroad depot, commandeered a locomotive and cars, and were on their way back to Jefferson City as soon as the engine could build up a head of steam. They feared that Lyon was already hot on their heels, so they paused at the Gasconade and Osage rivers to fire the railroad bridges and pull down the telegraph line, which Price evidently accomplished with his own hands. The party arrived back at the capital at two in the morning and immediately set to work drafting a proclamation to the people of the state. Anything but pithy and to the point, the document droned on for pages detailing the outrages perpetrated upon the citizenry by the federal government while the state had done nothing but seek peace. In it, the governor called for 50,000 state militia to join his ranks, repel invasion, and protect the lives, liberties, and property of the citizens of the state. He sounded the dire alarm that their enemies, the minions of the federal government, were already putting their diabolical schemes into action: "They are energetically hastening the execution of their bloody and revolutionary schemes for the inauguration of civil war in your midst; for the military occupation of your State by armed bands of lawless invaders; for the overthrow of your state government, and the subversion of those liberties, which that Government has always sought to protect. ... I earnestly exhort all good citizens of Missouri to rally under the flag of their State, for the protection of their homes and firesides, and for the defense of their most sacred rights and dearest privileges."

The main objects of his attack, Lyon and Blair, hardly considered themselves to be the lawless invaders described by Jackson. If secession amounted to treason, it was Jackson and Price and their followers who were operating outside of the framework of the government created by the founding fathers. Still, Jackson measured his foes correctly when he concluded that they intended to overthrow his government. Federal military occupation of the state also figured into Lyon and Blair's strategy. Already the aggressive Federal commanders were making plans to occupy what parts of the state they could in the short term—strategic river towns and railheads. And they fully intended to crush or drive from the state the gathering military forces of Jackson and Price. Lyon and Blair had no intention to relax the pressure they were applying to the secessionists for a single minute; if they had their way, when the dust settled, Missouri would be won for the Union.

Lyon and Blair immediately assembled an expeditionary force of Regular Army infantry and artillery along with Home Guard volunteers, embarking them on transports for the 145-mile journey up the Missouri River to Jefferson City. Before they departed, Lyon ordered three regiments of volunteers to proceed via train to Rolla and secure the railhead of the South West Branch of the Pacific Railroad. Command of this force came to rest with Col. Franz Sigel, a German revolutionary who fled to the United States and ended up in St. Louis. Sigel had orders to march from Rolla to Springfield along the old Indian trail turned state road. At Springfield, the key to southwestern Missouri, Sigel and his men could establish a Union presence in the region and a position from which to intercept Price and Jackson. Blair and Lyon rightly assumed that they could oust Jackson and Price from the Missouri River valley. They concluded that fleeing state officials and Missouri State Guard recruits would attempt to make their way down the western side of Missouri to join with Confederate forces in northwestern Arkansas and Indian Territory commanded by the hard-bitten Indian fighter, Mexican War hero, and Texas Ranger, Gen. Ben McCulloch. If Sigel placed his army to block Jackson and his still-unformed State Guard, Lyon could fall on Jackson's rear. Caught in the pincers of the Federal forces, the Missouri secessionist army would be crushed.

Just two days after the fateful Planter's House meeting, Lyon and Blair crowded their troops aboard three steamboats. The next day, June 15, Lyon and Blair landed their troops at Jefferson City to find the capital deserted. The governor and his cabinet, the General Assembly, and any State Guard forces that had been there had all left in evident haste with whatever records they could gather and carry with them. Lyon quickly learned that the State Guard, under Jackson's direct command, had fallen back to Boonville.

Jefferson City, with a large Unionist German-American population, was not a friendly place to make a stand against the federals. Boonville, however, was located in the heart of the Boonslick, a legendary Southern-settlement region, where Jackson and his men would receive a warm welcome from local residents. The town's commanding location on bluffs along the Missouri River was ideal for artillery batteries to block the Federal advance farther upstream. If Boonville could be held for only a few weeks, thousands of volunteers would be able to move down from north Missouri and cross the river at either Boonville or Lexington, the other gathering point for recruits. Anticipating the move to

Col. Franz Sigel was a German officer who fled to the United States after the Revolution of 1848 and ended up first in New York and then in St. Louis. When Lyon and Blair formed their volunteer regiments, Sigel became colonel of the Third Regiment. Before Lyon moved up the Missouri River to Jefferson City and Boonville, he sent Sigel to southwest Missouri to close any Rebel escape routes in that direction.
John Bradbury Collection

An Indian fighter, Mexican War hero, and Texas Ranger, Gen. Ben McCulloch led the Confederate forces in northwestern Arkansas and Indian Territory. Blair and Lyon suspected that fleeing state officials would try to make their way down the western side of Missouri to join forces with McCulloch.
Used by permission, State Historical Society of Missouri, Columbia

In this engraving of Jefferson City, the riverfront (now Jefferson Landing State Historic Site) is shown with the capitol in the background. On June 15, 1861, for the only time in the state's history, a legally elected government was deposed, and many of its officials were sent into exile. A provisional government then governed for the remainder of the Civil War. *Jefferson City—On the Missouri River* Engraved for Herrmann J. Meyer, New York, unknown date

Col. Henry Boernstein and three companies of men were dropped off at Jefferson City on June 15 to occupy the city and restore order. Blair's only instructions were to use his own judgment. In the absence of any government, he found himself exercising the powers of a provisional governor. *Missouri Historical Society, St. Louis*

Boonville, Jackson had ordered the state armory and its meager stores relocated to the fairgrounds on the east margin of the city. But Jackson never received the luxury of even one week to prepare. Lyon gave him scarcely more than three days. Col. Henry Boernstein and three companies secured Jefferson City while Lyon and Blair reembarked the remaining 1,700 men onto the steamboats and continued the pursuit in the direction of Boonville, fifty miles up the river. They tied off at nightfall several miles short of their destination. The next day, June 17, Lyon landed briefly at Rocheport. Local citizens informed him that the State Guard held the river bluffs ahead, possibly with artillery. Lyon determined to approach Boonville by land. At seven in the morning, he landed eight miles below Boonville, marched his soldiers across the floodplain, and began the ascent into the river hills on Rocheport Road that led to Boonville. Somewhere in front of him, Lyon believed, as many as 4,000 Guardsmen were waiting to fight Missouri's first battle of the Civil War and one of the first battles in the nation. The Battle of Bull Run, commonly called the first battle of the Civil War, was still five weeks off. When it came to fighting, Missourians liked to get off to an early start.

Jackson hardly had the force Lyon feared. The 50,000 men summoned in the governor's clarion call to arms never materialized despite Southerners making up the majority of Missouri's population. In fact, only about 1,500 volunteers appeared at Camp Bacon, the State Guard mustering area a few miles east of Boonville, and there was no time to drill or to equip this motley force properly. Those recruits with weapons mostly carried their own shotguns or squirrel rifles, not military-issue muskets. The temporary state armory at Boonville consisted of a couple of unmounted cannons (trophies from the Mexican War) and a variety of obsolete muskets from previous eras that were being retrofitted by Quartermaster Gen. James Harding. Most of these would soon be in Lyon's hands. The State Guard's only functional artillery battery, comprised of the four six-pounder brass cannons taken earlier from Liberty Arsenal, had been sent to Tipton along the Pacific Railroad and was not available for

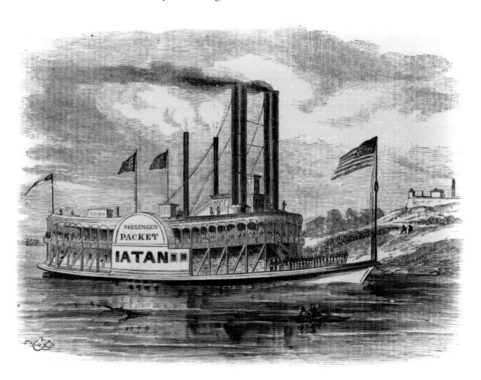

On June 15, the steamboat Iatan landed at the Jefferson City riverfront and unloaded three hundred Union soldiers to begin military occupation of the state capital. *Harper's Weekly*

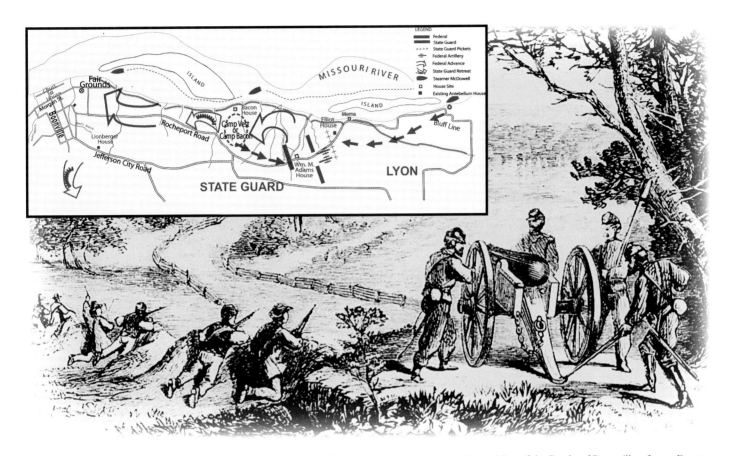

the impending fight. This was just as well, for none of the new recruits at Boonville knew how to man an artillery battery.

The State Guard commander, Maj. Gen. Sterling Price, was not present at Boonville; he had gone on to Lexington where Brigadier Generals William Y. Slack and James S. Rains had collected 3,000 troops. Jackson and Price never intended Boonville to be more than a delaying engagement while they gathered troops for a stand at Lexington. However, once Boonville was lost, as it almost certainly would be, the forces assembled at Lexington would be in jeopardy. Already a Federal cordon was being tightened around them. Maj. Samuel Sturgis and two regiments of Kansas infantry were moving eastward into Missouri to cut off a southward retreat, and Col. Samuel Curtis was said to be heading down from Iowa. Lyon's force was, of course, the most immediate threat. If Lyon prevailed at Boonville as expected, Price would have to direct Rains and his men southward while he rode ahead to beseech help from Gen. Bart Pearce's force of 2,000 Arkansas state troops and Ben McCulloch's 2,700 Confederates. The plan was for the converging columns of Jackson and Rains to link up at Lamar, north of Carthage, while Price persuaded the Confederates to combine their armies with his for a joint movement in Missouri to repel the Yankee invaders and redeem the state.

Meanwhile, at Boonville, Jackson assumed the mantle of commander in chief of the forces marshaled there. He knew he would not be able to hold Lyon back with his inexperienced and outgunned collection of men, but he was not going to quit his beloved Boonslick homeland without a fight. Jackson's second in command was his twenty-eight-year-old nephew, John Sappington Marmaduke. Only weeks before, this young West Point-trained, mid-Missouri blue blood had been a U. S. Army lieutenant on the Western frontier. Now he was a colonel in the State Guard leading a hastily thrown-together regiment getting ready to fight the federal

Map of the Battle of Boonville. *James Denny* The Battle of Boonville, fought on June 17, 1861, was a small battle that had large consequences. *Thomas Knox, "Camp-Fire and Cotton-Field," Belock and Company, New York, 1865*

33

John Sappington Marmaduke, Jackson's nephew and second in command, tried to dissuade his uncle from fighting Lyon at Boonville. *Used by permission, State Historical Society of Missouri, Columbia*

government. He protested in vain to his uncle that they stood no chance here. He argued for a withdrawal south across the Osage River to Warsaw. It was a superior position to make a stand. Besides, the men would be better drilled by then, and reinforcements could come up from southern Missouri. Jackson would have none of this. He ordered Marmaduke to advance his regiment and prepare for battle. Jackson should have taken his nephew's advice more seriously, for he was about to orchestrate a disaster. As Thomas Snead said of the coming battle, "Insignificant as was this engagement in a military aspect, it was in fact a stunning blow to the Southern Rights people of the State, and one which did incalculable and unending injury to the Confederates."

Lyon's force consisted of three companies of Regular Army enlistees, Blair's First Missouri Regiment, nine companies of the Second Missouri Regiment, and Capt. James Totten's light artillery battery. His column had begun to march out of the river bottom into the hills when they received the first fire from enemy skirmishers. Pushing forward another mile, they encountered the main force of State Guardsmen—400 or 500 men positioned by Marmaduke along a lane where a brick house, a wheat field, a thicket of woods, and rail fences provided cover. Lyon sized up the enemy position, placed his artillery in the middle of his line flanked on both sides by infantry, and advanced.

The battle lasted only twenty minutes. Capt. James Totten's Regular Army artillery battery rained shot down upon the State Guardsmen and drove them from their shelters. As Lyon's troops advanced across open fields, the Guardsmen formed another line and unleashed what one reporter called a "galling fire," inflicting the few Northern casualties of the day. However, just as it seemed that a real battle might erupt, the Guardsmen broke before Lyon's superior firepower and numbers. The retreat soon turned to headlong flight. Meanwhile, one of Lyon's steamers with a heavy howitzer aboard had moved up the river. It began to shell the recruits at Camp Bacon, who fled without bothering to gather their belongings. All of their equipment and supplies fell into Lyon's hands, including twelve hundred pairs of shoes. A last stand at the fairgrounds was easily dislodged by more shelling from the river-based howitzer and the steady advance of Lyon's infantry. The temporary arsenal set up there was captured as well.

As Lyon triumphantly marched into Boonville to receive the surrender of the town from a delegation of local leaders, Jackson and his entourage were beating a hasty retreat at the opposite end of town. The skirmish at Boonville had been a disaster for Missouri's struggling Southern cause. Civil War historian Bruce Catton summarized the significance of what Lyon had accomplished: "This fight at Boonville, the slightest of skirmishes by later standards, was in fact a very consequential victory for the federal government. Governor Jackson had been knocked loose from the control of his state, and the chance that Missouri could be carried bodily into the Southern Confederacy had gone glimmering. Jackson's administration was now, in effect, a government-in-exile, fleeing down the roads toward the Arkansas border, a disorganized body that would need a great deal of help from Jefferson Davis's government before it could give any substantial help in return."

Nathaniel Lyon's stunning success caught up with him at Boonville. He had moved farther and faster than any other Civil War general at that point and had done it with a handful of Regular Army officers and men, a few thousand volunteers, and Frank Blair's considerable assistance. With his success at Boonville, Lyon accomplished his immediate strategic tasks. By securing the Missouri River, he controlled the rich recruiting grounds in the Missouri River heartland and the territory extending all the way to the Iowa line and denied recruits and resources to the fleeing forces of the

THE BATTLE OF BOONEVILLE, OR THE GREAT MISSOURI "LYON" HUNT.

dislodged state government.

Lyon had succeeded in dispersing the Missouri secessionists, occupying the state capital and the principal towns, and controlling the heart of the state's population and wealth. The psychological blow of this seemingly easy toppling of the secessionist government no doubt discouraged many potential recruits from flocking to the Southern banner. Had Lyon's campaign ended at Boonville, it would have been considered an unparalleled success. However, the aggressive New Englander never considered letting Governor Jackson and his secessionists escape without striking a decisive blow.

The first Federal occupation of out-state river towns began with the Lyon campaign. Much to the resentment of the local Southern populace, the occupying Federal forces were the alien "damned Dutch." At Jefferson City, Col. Henry Boernstein had three companies to defend the capital from enemies without and within, to regulate and inspect all river traffic, to protect the entire Pacific Railroad from St. Louis to Sedalia, and to establish some semblance of civil government. There were no functioning courts, no public works, and no way to collect taxes. In the absence of a state government, the German-American officer functioned as provisional military governor. At this early stage, there were no precedents to guide his actions. Frank Blair told him, "Don't worry about any instructions, act in keeping with the circumstances and your own best judgment!" This the earnest and patriotic Boernstein did, though he was not a military man. His men were

In this cartoon, Lyon sends Governor Jackson, dressed in women's clothing, fleeing for his life with a subordinate. As a result of this victory, Lyon became a darling of the northern war press. *Library of Congress*

35

Capt. Hiram Bledsoe and his legendary Mexican War prize brass cannon, Old Sacramento, joined members of the State Guard as they evacuated Lexington to link up with Jackson and Price in southern Missouri. Bledsoe and his artillery battery would be employed in every major battle fought by the State Guard in the coming months. *Missouri Historical Society, St. Louis*

Susan Arnold McCausland was a high-spirited young bride from Virginia when, on July 9 at Lexington, she defied Union Col. Charles Stifel and his cadre of German-American St. Louisians. She boldly refused to take down a secession flag in her yard. A confrontation ensued. *File Photo, Missouri Department of Natural Resources*

quartered in the senate chamber of the capitol while the colonel took up quarters in the governor's mansion. So hastily had the Jackson family decamped that all of their furniture was still there—sheet music still rested on the piano. Short on troops to fulfill all his tasks, Boernstein soon organized Home Guards from Cole and the neighboring counties. Again, many of the men for these units were drawn from the local German-American population.

Local secessionists, who a week before had been flaunting Confederate flags and intimidating their Unionist neighbors, now discovered that no disloyalty would be tolerated by the new Federal regime. Boernstein immediately arrested five of the most vocal secessionists and imprisoned them in the cellars of the capitol without charges or due process. It was enough to suppress overt expressions of disloyalty among the capital city's population. The five citizens became the first among thousands of Missourians compelled to sign loyalty oaths in order to gain their freedom and maintain residence in occupied territory.

Three weeks after the fall of Boonville, while Lyon pursued Jackson southward, the first Federal detachment landed at the Lexington riverfront on July 9 and marched into town to establish control of this hotbed of secessionism. Hostilities between the opposing factions had been going on for two months by the time the Federals took control of Lexington. In mid-May, local secessionists had broken up a Unionist meeting and shot a German-American citizen in the leg. A little more than a month later, at Rock Creek in western Lafayette County, local militia clashed with Capt. Samuel Sturgis's Regular Army dragoons from Fort Leavenworth. On June 25, the State Guard regiments, who had been camped on the grounds of the Masonic College, moved out to link up with Jackson in southwest Missouri. With them was an artillery battery commanded by Capt. Hiram Bledsoe, who had in his possession a brass cannon captured at the Battle of Sacramento during the Mexican War. Bored out at a local foundry to become a twelve-pounder affectionately dubbed "Old Sac," the gun would be employed to deadly effect in every major battle fought by the State Guard in the coming months.

The Federals who had landed on the Lexington riverfront on July 9 consisted of Col. Charles Stifel and a regiment of German-American St. Louisians. As they marched into Lexington, they passed a house where Susan McCausland, a well-born newlywed from Virginia, flew a homemade secession flag in her yard. A confrontation between the German colonel, with his thick accent, and this spirited and beautiful young Southern woman ensued. Her hotblooded husband soon showed up with an old shotgun to defend her honor but was immediately arrested. He was the first citizen arrested for disloyalty in the predominantly Southern town. Federal authorities soon assembled two Home Guard companies from the local German-American population.

While at Boonville, Lyon made preparations for the next phase of his campaign. He intended to drive the secessionist forces not only out of Missouri but also out of Arkansas. Lyon's desire for a decisive confrontation was not necessarily unfounded. Swiftness and relentlessness are key to operations against insurgents, and the Missouri State Guard—barely organized, untrained, and poorly armed— was already routed and running. Besides, no one expected the war to last much longer than the summer. But Lyon had only 1,700 men. Reinforcements from St. Louis or Fort Leavenworth were days away. His hurried arrangements for supply and transportation could not keep pace with his ambition to destroy Governor Jackson's fugitive army.

Still, he had to have men and supplies. His hasty pursuit of Jackson to Boonville had been accomplished without an adequate supply train, but it was a necessity if his army was to move south and catch up with the state forces. However, Lyon experienced opposition from the rear by moderate Unionists working to circumscribe his actions, and his requisitions were not being filled in St. Louis. Adding insult to injury, Federal Quartermaster Justus McKinstry cancelled Lyon's arrangements for wagons and discharged his teamsters at St. Louis on the basis of the irregularity of the paperwork. Lyon combed the countryside around Boonville for transport, but the State Guard had already confiscated the best wagons and teams. Still, he managed to scrounge enough carts to meet his transport needs.

His greater need was for troops. Capt. Thomas Sweeny was on his way to Springfield with 360 soldiers, and Maj. Samuel Sturgis was moving toward the Osage River with 2,100 men. Once combined with his own force of 2,350 troops, Lyon would have an army of more than 4,500 soldiers, but not nearly enough to accomplish his goals. If State Guard forces linked up with the Confederates in Arkansas and Indian Territory, a large force of 15,000 to 20,000 men might be marshaled to meet Lyon.

There was no shortage of Union soldiers who might have been sent to Lyon. Henry Boernstein assessed the situation: "Volunteer regiments were under arms everywhere in Illinois, Wisconsin, Iowa, and Kansas, and an order from Washington would have brought all these eager troops to Missouri. Such numerical superiority alone would have been enough to drive the secessionist gangs out of Missouri, to expel the Rebels from Arkansas, and to bring the entire right bank of the Mississippi with its tributaries into the possession of the Union. But none of that happened. These troops were held inactive in their states for months, and they were then sent to places that needed them much less than sorely pressed Missouri."

For the magnitude of what the dynamic duo of Lyon and Blair had accomplished, their star was about to desert them. Their grand strategy was to be crushed by political intrigue, bad decisions, missed opportunities, and a string of blunders leading to military defeats that cast a pall of gloom over the Union cause. The Confederate movement in the West was soon to gain new energy, and the gate to the invasion of Missouri was to swing wide open. Faltering secessionist dreams in the state would be rekindled and the spirits of Southerners reanimated by new and deadly energy. The revival would feed the ever-expanding and increasingly all-encompassing Civil War that many had predicted would be over in six months.

The reverses for Lyon and Blair began shortly after Boonville. First, they learned that Missouri had been absorbed into the Department of Ohio. Their new commander, Maj. Gen. George B. McClellan, four hundred miles away in Cincinnati, didn't even have a detailed Missouri map. Fighting political and bureaucratic battles instead of secessionists, McClellan tacitly approved Lyon's course of action, but Lyon still lacked reinforcements, supplies, and transportation. Missouri's conservatives in Washington, men like Attorney General Edward Bates, had persuaded Lincoln and Cmd. Gen. Winfield Scott that Lyon was too brash to continue directing affairs in Missouri. His aggressive methods might alienate moderate slaveholding Conditional Unionists in Missouri and cause the delicate balance in Missouri and Kentucky to teeter toward disunion. Lyon needed a defender in Washington, and Blair was ideally positioned to take up that role.

Blair had won a seat in the House of Representatives in the same election that brought Jackson and Lincoln to office. He had a choice between continuing in the military campaign he and Lyon had laid out or going to Washington to use his influence to remove political obstacles and support Lyon with the men and

Brig. Gen. Thomas "Fighting Tom" Sweeny was Irish-born and arrived in America at age twelve. He came to St. Louis as a lieutenant in January 1861 but proved so useful to Lyon and Blair that he was a brigadier general of volunteers by May. After the Battle of Boonville, he was given the assignment of moving on Springfield in pursuit of retreating pro-secessionist elements of the former state government and its State Guard.
Library of Congress

With the appointment of Maj. Gen. John Charles Frémont, the famous Pathfinder of the West, to command the Department of Missouri, Nathaniel Lyon's frustrations in gaining support from his superiors should have been relieved. Instead, Frémont showed little interest in Lyon's plight and concentrated his concern on perceived threats of invasion in southeast Missouri rather than going after Price in southwest Missouri. *Library of Congress*

supplies he so desperately needed. Blair decided the best course was to take his Congressional seat. The remarkable team of Blair and Lyon that had accomplished so much in the first six months of 1861 was now dissolved. Neither would be as effective in directing the future affairs of Missouri as they had been when together they boldly drove the forces of disunion before them and preserved Missouri for the Union.

The worst blow to Lyon was to fall shortly when a man who should have been a close ally and supporter, John C. Frémont, was appointed to command a newly created Department of the West. The Blair family worked hard to secure this disastrous appointment. For their efforts, they would see their well-laid plans completely dashed and witness the undoing of a great deal of what they had accomplished in Missouri.

CHAPTER 3

The Battle of Carthage

BY THE BEGINNING of July, Lyon finally managed to cobble together a supply train, then he was dealt another setback—this time by Mother Nature. As if cooperating with the enemy, the heavens opened on June 26. Torrential rains flooded the Osage and Grand rivers and nearly put a stop to all land travel. Mired in mud and blocked by flooding streams, Lyon found himself immobilized at Boonville as his enemy slipped away. One small consolation for his frustrations was that he was now a celebrity. Lyon had become the darling of the Northern war press by the time he marched from Boonville on July 3 to resume his campaign.

Meanwhile, the secessionists were trying to put as many miles as possible between themselves and the Union force. Demoralized by their drubbing at Boonville and with Jackson suffering from cancer that would soon kill him, the group of 1,500 militiamen, state officials, and wagons filled with state records moved rapidly toward southwestern Missouri in what both sides dubbed the "Boonville Races."

Jackson's forces withdrew southwestward through Tipton in the direction of Cole Camp. The town was a potential obstruction to the army's flight. Despite being in a Southern settlement region, Cole Camp had a sizable population of German immigrants who, along with a number of old stock settlers, formed a significant block of support for the Union. They had formed themselves into a large Home Guard force and had received some four hundred muskets from the St. Louis arsenal, but they had little powder. About four hundred members of this unit were encamped on a farm east of Cole Camp on the night of June 18-19; many of the men were sleeping in two barns. Despite receiving warnings that secessionists only twenty miles away at Warsaw were planning an attack, the Home Guard camp was not placed on a state of alert. Some 350 local State Guardsmen led by Capt. (soon to be Lt. Col.) Walter S. O'Kane struck the unwary Home Guards at three in the

Col. Franz Sigel hoped to be the anvil to Lyon's hammer, but the Missouri State Guard forced him into a fighting retreat that swirled through the streets of Carthage before the battle ended.
Andy Thomas

39

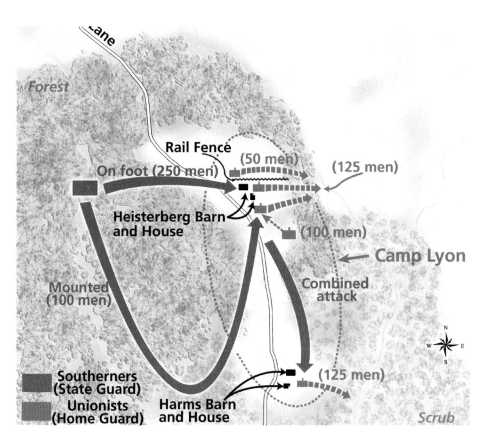

Walter S. O'Kane's Missouri State Guardsmen struck German-American Home Guards sleeping in barns near Cole Camp. The victory was a gratifying retaliation for German contributions to the Union cause. *James M. Denny, Missouri Department of Natural Resources*

morning. Screaming "No mercy for the Dutch!" they poured a hail of rifle fire at point-blank range into one of the barns filled with sleeping volunteers. About 35 Home Guards were killed and some 60 wounded in this vicious clash of neighbors. O'Kane's men rode off with 350 of the Home Guard's muskets, a welcome and needed commodity. Not only did the State Guardsmen get the satisfaction of dealing out some payback for the damage that Germans had done at Camp Jackson and Boonville, they had also gained their first victory against the Federal forces.

Reinforcements and recruits joined Jackson's column en route, including some of those captured and paroled at Camp Jackson in St. Louis. Important among the latter group were the experienced artillerists Henry Guibor and William P. Barlow. At last there were officers who knew how to employ the battery of four cannons seized at the Liberty Arsenal. Jackson's army got lucky when it crossed the Osage River at Warsaw before the rains came. In alternating torrential rains and scorching heat, the weary secessionists eventually marched unmolested to a junction on July 3 with Gen. James S. Rains's force of 3,000 men at Lamar.

Lyon could only hope Jackson's flight to the far southwestern corner of Missouri might yet be blocked by troops he had sent there simultaneously with his advance to Jefferson City. Capt. Thomas Sweeny, a dependable Regular Army officer, commanded this wing of the Union advance, sometimes styled the "Southwest Expedition." The brigade of five mostly German regiments was to intercept Governor Jackson's Missourians and hold them for Lyon, block Confederate incursion from Arkansas, and secure the region's valuable lead mines at Granby. It was a tall order for the one-armed Mexican War veteran, who remained behind in St. Louis arranging for supplies while the first troops, clad in neat "militia-gray" uniforms, took to the field under command of Col. Franz Sigel. A veteran of the failed revolution in Europe in 1848, a mathematics professor, and a popular figure in the German community in St. Louis, Sigel began his prominent and controversial

career by putting his men on trains to Rolla, the end of the tracks of the South West Branch of the Pacific Railroad. His troops dispersed a squad of local secessionists there on June 14, seized the courthouse and railroad facilities, and hurried down the state road to Springfield, the key to all of southwestern Missouri. Sigel probed as far as Sarcoxie by the end of June before learning not only that Missourians under Sterling Price and Ben McCulloch's Confederate troops were nearby but also that Governor Jackson's army was still north of Carthage. Sigel posted a company at Neosho, then with commendable boldness turned his small main force northward toward Jackson. He still hoped to become the anvil to Lyon's hammer, crushing the rebellion between them. But now the possibility also existed that the forces of Price-McCulloch and Jackson might end up being the hammer and anvil that crushed Sigel.

On July 4, Governor Jackson and Gen. Mosby Monroe Parsons learned that Sigel's men were in Carthage. Slowed by muddy roads, the opposing forces converged the next day, nine miles north of Carthage. On the brow of a prairie ridge, Jackson, who had assumed command, arrayed his army in line of battle to await the arrival of Sigel. He now had 6,000 men with him, all dedicated to the Southern cause and eager to fight. But only 4,375 had weapons, and these men composed the battle line. Although the Second, Third, Fourth, and Sixth divisions of the Missouri State Guard were on the field, none of these divisions were up to full troop strength. The

Missouri State Guard cavalry got between
the Union infantry and Col. Franz Sigel's
baggage train at the crossing of Buck Branch,
forcing Sigel to attack to save his wagons.
Andy Thomas

men had no uniforms and few military rifles. Powder and ammunition were in short supply. Still, they outnumbered Sigel four to one and could almost match Sigel in artillery; Sigel had eight cannons to their seven. Jackson's army also had the large advantage of possessing cavalry. Their 1,358 mounted troops alone outnumbered their enemy's entire force, while Sigel had no cavalry of any kind. Sigel did have the advantage of commanding men who carried government-issued muskets and had some training. Jackson's men, by contrast, had received little by way of drill or military discipline. Jackson also lacked officers with military experience who could turn undisciplined men into soldiers. Jackson's entourage also included a number of state political leaders and a wagon caravan of official documents and personal effects for the government-in-exile that Jackson was soon to establish.

With the State Guard dead ahead, Sigel and his 1,100 well-disciplined soldiers forded Dry Fork Creek. They then advanced three-quarters of a mile to the crest of a small hill, where the Federal force deployed for battle in the face of a ragged, mile-long line of secessionists. The two sides then commenced an artillery duel that lasted perhaps an hour before Jackson ordered his mounted Missourians to move around either side of Sigel's line and attack him in flank and rear. Sigel realized he was dangerously exposed. To make matters worse, his unprotected baggage train of thirty-two wagons lagged some distance behind. Sigel immediately ordered a retreat.

As Sigel's force crossed back over Dry Fork Creek, an artillery battery and five companies of infantry were left concealed behind the trees on the elevated ground of the creek's south side. Jackson's infantry advanced to within four hundred yards of this position before Sigel's rear guard opened fire. The artillerists and riflemen stalled the attack of Jackson's infantry for two hours and inflicted the heaviest casualties of the battle. Finally, the rear guard gave ground under the pressure of the superior numbers of the State Guard infantry.

In the meantime, two State Guard cavalry regiments managed to circle around Sigel's column to form a blockade at Buck Branch Creek. They were positioned between Sigel's column and his supply train, which still lagged to the rear. The tables were now turned, and Sigel became the attacker. His infantry scattered the enemy horsemen with a bayonet charge, crossed Buck Branch, and regained his baggage train. Sigel then skillfully positioned his troops and artillery on all sides of the baggage train and continued the retreat toward Carthage, all the while successfully fending off attempts by the State Guard forces to attack his flanks.

The result was a fighting retreat running nearly nine miles to Carthage. There were "stands" at stream crossings along the way and fighting in the streets of the town before Sigel was able to disengage at nightfall. The Battle of Carthage resulted in 244 total casualties. Sigel suffered 13 killed and 31 wounded; Jackson sustained 30 killed and 125 wounded. While this toll was modest when compared with the casualty lists of the terrible battles to follow, the Battle of Carthage was one of the bloodiest confrontations of this early stage in the Civil War. It was widely reported in newspapers, North and South, before the Battle of Bull Run (Manassas), Virginia, on July 21 took over the headlines.

The action at Carthage, also known as Dry Fork, demonstrated Sigel's ability as an artillerist but also his propensity to blunder into near disaster. His artillery, a few subordinate officers, and the stout hearts of his German soldiers saved him at Carthage. His men, as well as their enemy counterparts, deserved better commanders. The same day at Neosho, Ben McCulloch's cavalry gobbled up the company Sigel left behind—a bloodless capture and the first action involving Confederate troops on Missouri soil.

CHAPTER 4

The Battle of Wilson's Creek

$\mathscr{S}$IGEL FAILED TO ACHIEVE his primary objective when the Missouri State Guard brushed him aside, joined Sterling Price's men, and established a large encampment at Cowskin Prairie, only a few miles from Missouri's borders with Arkansas and the Indian Territory. By the time Thomas Sweeny's reinforcements arrived from Rolla and Lyon's army arrived at Springfield, the Union army numbered about 5,800 officers and men but no longer retained the tactical advantage.

Price had gathered about 10,000 men within distance of Confederate help, and the Missouri leaders recovered their nerve as an army began to coalesce. But several thousand recruits lacked any weapons at all, and there had been mixed success at getting Confederate help. Although Ben McCulloch and his Arkansas counterpart, Gen. Bart Pearce, loaned the Missourians several hundred muskets, they were unimpressed with the secessionist "army." Cooperation with Governor Jackson's Missourians was complicated by the fact that, while Arkansas had officially joined the Confederacy in May, Missouri was still officially part of the Union.

And there were practical reasons for doubt. The Missouri army was still a disorganized, beggarly mob, theoretically organized into divisions but operating more like an impoverished county court than a military force. It was bereft of experienced leaders, organization, discipline, supplies, arms, and ammunition—in fact, everything but horses. However, General McCulloch underestimated the mettle of the Guardsmen, who demonstrated considerable improvisation as they rolled Granby lead and powder into cannon cartridges, cut blacksmith iron into shrapnel, and yearned for the day when they would blast the hated Federals from Missouri soil.

Unfortunately for the Missourians, McCulloch and Price developed a mutual antipathy to each other that compromised their military efficiency. Missouri political

The combined Southern force might have struck Lyon first had not a summer shower threatened to dissolve the cartridges in the pockets of the men. Instead, they went into camp along Wilson's Creek, where Lyon's forces attacked them the next day. *Andy Thomas*

Already renowned as a Texas Ranger, Brig. Gen. Ben McCulloch led the first Confederate army into Missouri. Unfortunately, McCulloch and Sterling Price could not get along, compromising their victory at Wilson's Creek. *John Bradbury Collection*

envoys to Richmond fared no better, alienating President Jefferson Davis, who remembered the double-dealing and untrustworthy behavior Price and Jackson demonstrated by the ill-fated Price-Harney Agreement. These personal antagonisms ultimately affected Missouri's destiny. Although McCulloch became convinced that the best option was to beat Lyon in Missouri, he and Price disagreed on the method and command. As their combined forces (about 15,000 men) ate up the countryside, the generals quarreled for a month. In circumstances that remain in dispute, they finally agreed at the end of July to a combined advance against Lyon, with McCulloch commanding the Missourians under Price, Pearce's Arkansas state troops, and his own Louisiana and Texas Confederates. They could not agree on a name—the Army of the West or Western Army has become the preferred designation for this unusual combination of Confederate and state troops.

As if to underscore the ambiguity that existed in Missouri from beginning to end, Lyon's combined Federal force at Springfield was also known in the press at that time as the Army of the West. The men were mostly volunteers from Missouri, Iowa, and Kansas with a strong core of U.S. Regular Army infantrymen and artillerists led by West Point-trained officers (later generals) Samuel Sturgis, John M. Schofield, Frederick Steele, and James S. Totten. Lyon also had the considerable assistance of one-armed Thomas Sweeny (the former captain was now a general of short-term volunteers) and the enthusiastic but questionable counsel of Franz Sigel. The troops were still mostly inexperienced and their regimental leadership not much better than the Rebels, but as a whole, the men were better organized and trained, carried better arms, and were willing to fight. Sweeny sallied from Springfield as far south as Forsyth. His artillery shelled the Taney County courthouse as the infantry secured the town and Missouri State Guard supplies cached there. Casualties were minimal; the troops celebrated by looting the town's businesses—even the chaplain of the First Iowa Infantry took a share of the plunder. One of the worst wounded was newspaper correspondent Franc Wilkie, hit by friendly fire. Other journalists took part in the action, firing their pistols at the enemy across the White River. Their readers never learned that the expedition to Forsyth was a meaningless victory at a cost of sweat and shoe leather.

The reality was that Lyon's army was outnumbered by at least three to one, and the enlistments of many of his volunteers were about to expire. The soldiers lived on half and quarter rations, remained on constant alert, and responded to alarms from all quarters. There were severe shortages of wagons, equipment, forage for horses, and tents. Like their enemy counterparts, the men lived off the land like deer. More than two hundred miles from St. Louis and one hundred from the railhead at Rolla, Lyon's army reached the end of its logistical tether. Only a trickle of supplies reached Springfield, but Lyon and his soldiers did get a new department commander, John C. Frémont.

The son-in-law of Sen. Thomas Hart Benton, Frémont was already famous as the "Pathfinder" of the Rocky Mountain West, protégé of the Blair family, and the first Republican candidate for president in 1856. He seemed to be a perfect candidate for the job. President Lincoln commissioned him a major general in the Regular Army and gave him a free hand in Missouri. Frémont did not reach St. Louis until July 25 and demonstrated little concern for Lyon's plight. Once in St. Louis, he surrounded himself with eastern and foreign military advisors, cronies from the West, a personal bodyguard of cavalry, and maps of the Mississippi River valley, not southwestern Missouri.

The ruin of Frémont's reputation began in St. Louis with his failure to recognize the advantages of supporting Lyon and consolidating his gains. In his defense, his

Missouri command was still chaotic, and following the Union defeat in Virginia at Bull Run, he would get no help from the War Department. Frémont's first concern was, as it should have been, Union control of the mouth of the Ohio River at Cairo, Illinois. Confederates from Arkansas and Tennessee threatened this critical point, and fledgling Missouri State Guard organizations in southeastern Missouri might have opened the way to assault St. Louis. Overestimating the threat to Cairo, Frémont led his meager reserves downriver, not to Springfield.

Lyon was left to his own devices. Worn out by the accumulated stresses of command and without support from Frémont, he began to make bad choices. When he learned that the much larger enemy army was moving toward Springfield, retreat to Rolla became the only realistic option. Most of his West Point subordinates agreed but also shared Lyon's desire to strike a blow before withdrawing and were loath to leave southwestern Missouri Unionists to the mercies of the secessionists. Ever aggressive, Sweeny urged a fight to the "last cartridge and bit of mule flesh" before retreating. Lyon and his officers ultimately determined to try to cripple the enemy before withdrawing. It was a risky but not unreasonable decision, but only if the Union army remained compact and moved quickly. Lyon missed an opportunity on August 2 when he marched down Wire Road and routed James S. Rains's advancing Missouri cavalry at Dug Spring. He might have given up then after marching back to Springfield, but Lyon decided on one last attempt. This decision sealed his fate, but his big mistake was letting himself be talked into a

Had Nathaniel Lyon's campaign ended at Boonville, it would have been considered a success. He pressed his luck too far at Wilson's Creek. *John Bradbury Collection*

An Irish-born veteran of the Mexican War and Regular Army officer, Thomas Sweeny led the Southwest Expedition and the Forsyth raid. *Library of Congress*

Franz Sigel talked Lyon into letting him lead an independent flanking attack on the Rebel encampment at Wilson's Creek. In southwest Missouri, this was one of Lyon's worst decisions. *Library of Congress*

Already slightly wounded twice by late morning, Lyon was leading a countercharge by Kansas Infantry when he was shot a third time and killed. *Library of Congress*

On facing page: Lyon's main force held "Bloody Hill," which overlooked the Rebel camps along Wilson's Creek, while Sigel's column swung south to attack from the rear. After initial success, the battle plan foundered when Sigel's men were routed. *Shaded relief map, National Park Service. Troop dispositions and movements, James M. Denny, Missouri Department of Natural Resources*

revised battle plan by Franz Sigel. The new plan featured Sigel in an independent role in which he would march his brigade (two German regiments, an artillery battery, and a company of Regular cavalry) around the enemy's rear to strike it from behind. The scheme was chancy at best and further reduced Lyon's already outnumbered main force. Lyon's confidence in Sigel turned out to be ill-advised.

With supplies and forage dwindling for 15,000 men, Southern forces also had to move quickly to seize the opportunity to destroy Lyon's army. After a bitter dispute between McCulloch and Price following "Rains's Scare," in which Brig. Gen. James S. Rains's men fled from Federal forces at Dug Springs, the Southern army moved north on Wire Road toward Springfield with Price's men in the advance. The Southern army might have struck first had it not been for a light rain on August 9 that threatened unprotected ammunition in the pockets of the troops. The result was an overnight bivouac along a stream called Wilson's Creek. Somehow, there were no picket guards posted around the camp, and in the morning as Price's and McCulloch's men began getting breakfast, Lyon's army began firing on them. Initially, the Union assault was another of Lyon's stunning surprises. His main force of 4,200 men attacked from the north, throwing the Missourians into chaos and setting wagons and tents afire with artillery shells. Sigel's operation also began well. He successfully brought his 1,200-man brigade and artillery battery undetected to a position in McCulloch's rear. He shelled the enemy cavalry out of their camps but then lost control of his troops, who had gone to looting the enemy encampment. While trying to regain control, Sigel allowed an unidentified force that he believed to be gray-clad Union soldiers (blue uniforms had not yet become the Northern standard) to come up unchallenged to within firing distance. The mystery troops, Louisiana soldiers sent by McCulloch as it turned out, unleashed a devastating volley

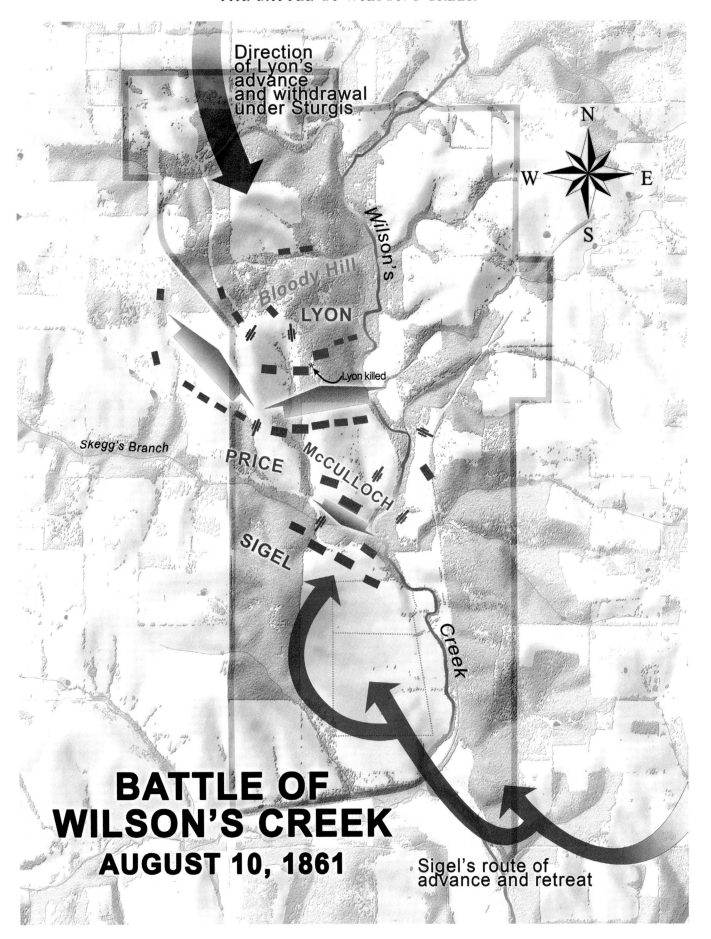

Direction of Lyon's advance and withdrawal under Sturgis

N
W   E
S

Wilson's

Bloody Hill

LYON

Lyon killed

Skegg's Branch

PRICE

McCULLOCH

SIGEL

Creek

BATTLE OF WILSON'S CREEK
AUGUST 10, 1861

Sigel's route of advance and retreat

before the mistake was realized. Ultimately they killed or captured a large part of Sigel's brigade, captured his artillery, and drove the remnants from the field. Sigel's brigade played no further part in the battle, and the German general abandoned his command. He was one of the first to return to Springfield—accompanied by only a single orderly.

Lyon never knew what became of Sigel but had stirred up a hornet's nest himself. Price's and McCulloch's men recovered well from their initial surprise. First with artillery fire and then with gathering numbers of infantrymen, Louisiana and Arkansas soldiers drove back Lyon's eastern flank as Price's Missourians blocked the center of the Union advance on a hill overlooking the camps in the Wilson's Creek valley. The low, brush-covered eminence, known afterward as Bloody Hill, became the focus of the battle. Lyon stabilized his line along the brow of the hill. He placed his Missouri, Iowa, and Kansas infantry volunteers in line, backed them with his artillery (manned by Regular Army officers and men), and forced his enemy to come to him.

The Missourians obliged whenever a captain or company officer corralled a group of men long enough to launch a charge uphill into the brush and the muzzles of the Yankee guns. It wasn't quite hand-to-hand fighting, but it was within shotgun range (the hunting weapons were a common Missouri firearm at this time), which was close and deadly enough. Brush and gunpowder smoke obscured vision; there were instances of mistaken identity on both sides. Price gradually formed a fighting line with the infantry divisions of Slack, Parsons, and Clark; McBride's division of Ozarkers made a fierce slashing attack before mid-morning. Price pushed more and more men toward the Yankees as the day wore on. After finishing with Sigel, McCulloch's Confederates joined the Missourians.

Price and McCulloch ultimately brought about three times Lyon's number of men into battle, launching increasingly violent general assaults on the Yankee line before being driven back. Both sides gained and lost ground, but the Rebels threatened to swamp Lyon's army. His volunteers fought well, but there were terrible casualties among his infantry, and ammunition was running low. Regular Army artillerymen led by profane, alcoholic James S. Totten saved the Union army from utter destruction, knocking back Missourians, Arkansawyers, Louisianans, and Texans with sprays of canister, breaking up Rebel concentrations and driving away enemy cavalry threatening Union flanks.

There was a furious Southern assault about mid-morning. Price and Lyon even spotted one another, and Lyon may have rashly considered personal combat before calling up a regiment of Kansas infantry in his last reserve. Masked in blood from earlier slight wounds to the head and foot, Lyon led the Kansans in a countercharge. As he advanced, he suffered his third and final wound of the day—a bullet through the heart. It was not yet noon; combat had been in progress for more than six hours under a brutal sun. Command devolved on Maj. Samuel Sturgis, who reorganized his men and repulsed yet another ferocious combined Southern onslaught. With casualties increasing, ammunition running low, and no more water for his thirsty men, Sturgis ordered the inevitable withdrawal during the next lull in the fighting, surprising some of his own men who yet held their lines and who did not consider themselves beaten. The Union army slipped away to Springfield in good order, taking up most of their wounded, although Lyon's corpse was left behind in the confusion. It was the Southerners' turn to be surprised when they advanced through the brush to the top of Bloody Hill again, only to find the enemy's positions abandoned. Most soldiers in both armies probably would have agreed with the comment of Gen. Bart Pearce of Arkansas, who said of the

enemy, "We were happy to see them go."

Wilson's Creek (known in the Southern press as Oak Hills and Springfield) was one of the costliest battles of the Civil War. The Southern Army of the West held the field in victory, but at a terrible cost. It did not pursue the retreating foe. The men had been literally decimated—about one in ten was killed or wounded. Medical arrangements were virtually nonexistent; there were large numbers of wounded of both armies still untended on the battlefield and many bodies to be buried. The men in the Missouri State Guard divisions of Clark, McBride, Parsons, and Slack were the worst shot-up; General Price suffered a slight but painful flesh wound in his side. Arkansawyers and Confederates also shed blood at Wilson's Creek, contributing another tithe (almost 500 out of 5,000 men in the two brigades) to the Southern butcher's bill. The shaky organization of the Missouri State Guard reeled from serious casualties among its officers, including one of its most promising, Col. Richard Weightman, who died of earlier wounds as the battle ended. Ammunition and supplies were about gone, and petty disputes broke out over the distribution of loaned weapons, captured equipment, and battle honors. McCulloch still held the military capacity of Price and his Missourians in contempt. He should have known better by then, but he had valid concerns about his own authority in Missouri and his tenuous supply situation.

McCulloch and Price feuded over the next move. Each had different interests

Union forces retreated after a bullet killed Lyon. His body was forgotten in the confusion. It rested temporarily on John S. Phelps's farm before relatives collected it for burial in Connecticut. *Used by permission, State Historical Society of Missouri, Columbia*

Lyon was the first Union general to die in battle and one of the North's first war heroes. *Mourning card, John Bradbury Collection*

Franz Sigel's independent assault on the Southern camp began successfully, but he blundered badly by allowing unidentified troops to approach his lines. They proved to be McCulloch's Confederates, who broke up the German's ranks and captured 130 of his men and all of his artillery. Sigel's force played no further part at Wilson's Creek.
Used by permission, State Historical Society of Missouri, Columbia

and objectives. The Missourians understandably wanted to capitalize on their victory immediately by marching on the center of the state, reclaiming the most populous and prosperous part of the pro-secession heartland. McCulloch thought more about his supply problems and the extent of his authority to deal with Price. Ultimately he declined to cooperate with Price and marched his Confederates back to his base at Fort Smith, Arkansas; Bart Pearce also took his Arkansawyers home. But all of western Missouri was open to Price's Missourians. Before the leaves turned, they would surge northward to the Missouri River in what was the high tide of the Missouri State Guard.

The Federal forces abandoned Springfield the day after the Battle of Wilson's Creek. The army moved slowly toward Rolla in a column seven miles long, mixed in with a horde of panic-stricken Unionist refugees from southwestern Missouri. Soldiers and civilians alike were lucky that the Southerners were in no condition to harass them. Nearly one in four of the men in the Union army engaged at Wilson's Creek had been wounded or lay dead on the battlefield with Lyon. Lyon's body was taken to Springfield by Price and left there to be safeguarded by Mrs. John S. Phelps until relatives retrieved it for burial in Connecticut. The Federal First Kansas and First Missouri Infantry regiments lost more than a quarter of their number on Bloody Hill; this put them in the battered company of Union regiments with the greatest losses during the entire war. Like many of their Southern counterparts, Yankee officers had suffered grievously leading their men from the front.

There were fewer dead and wounded in Sigel's brigade, but 130 of his men were prisoners of war in Confederate hands. The worst Union wounded remained in temporary hospitals at Springfield. Those able to travel endured evacuation in jolting army wagons. Sigel led the retreat despite the disgrace of his brigade but relinquished command midway to Major Sturgis after what amounted to a revolt of the Regular Army officers, who blamed Sigel for Lyon's defeat as well as mismanagement of the retreat. However, an Iowa volunteer believed there was plenty of blame to go around among officers who failed their soldiers. He acknowledged his enemy's grit as well and imagined the demoralizing effect of having one assault after another go to ground in front of the Union line: "They fought well enough, but couldn't get anywhere. Their high officers were no good; they were like ours."

Amid recriminations, the army reached relative safety at the railhead at Rolla a week after the battle. By that time, the Northern war press had already tried to portray the defeat as victory, and in the lamented Lyon, the first Union general to be killed, created one of the North's earliest war heroes. But Lyon's Missouri strategy seemed as dead as its creator. Worse still, General Frémont in St. Louis did not seem to notice the disaster in southwestern Missouri or the tremendous enthusiasm it generated among secessionists in Missouri. The Pathfinder garnered much of the blame for Wilson's Creek—his refusal to support Lyon counted more against him than his headstrong subordinate's refusal to retreat.

Frémont had already begun to consolidate many of Lyon's strategic gains by fortifying St. Louis, reinforcing the railheads at Rolla and Pilot Knob, and concentrating other forces at Cairo, Illinois, and on the Mississippi shore at Bird's Point, Missouri. But Frémont's attention remained directed to the Mississippi Valley, notably the area where the Missouri and Arkansas deltas, Kentucky, and Tennessee meet along the river and where the Confederacy first blocked the way to the Gulf of Mexico. Gen. Leonidas Polk, Frémont's Confederate counterpart commanding the defenses of the upper Mississippi River, also realized the critical importance of the river. Moreover, two of his subordinates, politician turned general of Tennessee troops, Gideon Pillow, and the former mayor of St. Joseph, M. Jeff Thompson, schemed to use the Mississippi as the avenue by which they would reclaim all of southeastern Missouri.

Jeff Thompson, a truly colorful character of the war, gained a Missouri State Guard commission despite having called Governor Jackson a coward and a fool. He was headed in quest of a commission in his native Virginia when he washed up broke at Memphis before turning back toward Missouri via Pocahontas, Arkansas. He went to Doniphan, Missouri, where Missouri State Guard forces there elected him a lieutenant colonel. By an even more unlikely chain of events, Thompson was elected to command the First Division of the Missouri State Guard, in a district embracing southeastern Missouri from south of St. Louis to the Missouri Bootheel.

Thompson's swamp brigade of 2,000 to 3,000 men, as under-equipped and unarmed as any of Price's, operated most of the summer between Cape Girardeau and New Madrid and raided as far north as the river towns of Charleston (where Thompson relieved the bank of $57,000, giving his receipt to the board of directors), Commerce (where he fired a defiant artillery shot across the river into Illinois), and Lucas Bend (the site of a duel with gunboats) on the Mississippi. Encouraged by Governor Jackson, Thompson in Missouri and General Pillow in Tennessee hoped to enlist Gen. William H. Hardee, the Confederate commander in northeastern Arkansas, in combined operations in southeastern Missouri. A Southern advance would augment those in the southwest part of the state by McCulloch and Price. The rosiest Southern scenario envisioned the capture of St. Louis.

Unfortunately for Thompson's men, Generals Polk, Pillow, and Hardee cooperated no better than their colleagues in southwestern Missouri. Pillow argued for the capture of Cape Girardeau, with Hardee moving up into the interior of Missouri to attack Ironton and Pilot Knob. Although Hardee marched his badly

Former mayor of St. Joseph and secessionist firebrand, M. Jeff Thompson became a Missouri State Guard general in southeast Missouri despite his having called Governor Jackson a coward. *John Bradbury Collection*

There were signs that the war would not be brief and disturbing portents of disaster and hardship yet to come. Volunteers for both sides continued to enlist, seemingly more enthusiastic than ever despite the slaughter.

armed 3,000-man army to Greenville, Missouri, he refused to move on Ironton until the Iron Mountain Railroad, the Union lifeline from St. Louis, was captured or broken. Confederate superiors did not intervene in the impasse. Jeff Thompson, the only man apparently ready to do anything, rode ceaselessly between Bloomfield and Sikeston on the northern edge of the Missouri lowlands and to New Madrid and Belmont but accomplished little more than scouting for his immobile Confederate allies. The grand Southern offensive in southeastern Missouri never materialized. Instead it provoked retaliatory countermeasures by the Yankees, who had not heretofore ventured far into the region. Thompson's swamp brigade survived only by their leader's bluff and guile, soon to be tested by an obscure Illinois colonel named Ulysses S. Grant.

The momentous summer of 1861 ended with Union forces occupying all the key points in Missouri except Springfield, and most of the state was under nominal Union control. But the Missouri State Guard was victorious in southwestern Missouri; Jeff Thompson and his men were holding their own on the edge of the swamps in southeastern Missouri. Both sides had reason for optimism; both still believed that the war would end soon with a climactic battle.

But there were signs that the war would not be brief and disturbing portents of disaster and hardship yet to come. Volunteers for both sides continued to enlist, seemingly more enthusiastic than ever despite the slaughter. Recruiting, training, and equipping proceeded apace. There were many now who had stood under gunfire; officers and men began to learn their jobs. In the next round, the armies would be even tougher to defeat. The armies of both sides impressed or seized large amounts of personal property, mostly horses, livestock, food, and forage, and soldiers committed considerable petty theft as well as outright looting. The state's sovereignty and boundaries had been violated repeatedly by both Union and Confederate forces; local governments had mostly ceased to function. Banditry had begun to break out. No part of Missouri was free from disorder.

General Frémont officially declared martial law in Missouri following the disaster at Wilson's Creek, but military authorities, Northern and Southern, had already assumed tremendous powers. They arrested civilian sympathizers on the advice of neighborhood informants and forced men of military age into service despite their opinions or desire to serve. Outspoken Missourians began to be threatened, arrested, burned out, and killed for their sympathies. Confiscation of private property became widespread and with very little chance of recourse. The heavy-handedness of military men created legions of formerly neutral citizens with newfound grievances that were no longer mere political theory but actual injury. They were the first of what became thousands of refugees temporarily or permanently dispossessed from their homes in Missouri. Unionists congregated at St. Louis and the strongholds at Rolla and Ironton. Secessionists, in turn, headed for Kentucky, Arkansas, and Texas; many of them removed their most valuable property—slaves—to safer Confederate territory. Other slaves emancipated themselves wherever Union soldiers were present, beginning an exodus from slavery that never ended. Property rights and state sovereignty, precisely what Southerners had hoped to preserve, would never be the same in Missouri.

CHAPTER 5

A Tale of Two Governments

Missouri State Archives

WITH MISSOURI'S ELECTED government unseated and fleeing from Lyon's army, the state capitol stood vacant. Most of the machinery of government had ground to a complete halt. Union authorities faced a situation for which no precedent existed—the need to fabricate an entirely new government to direct the affairs of state. But how to fashion such a government and by what authority was a question for which there existed no neat, prepackaged answer. The governor and most of his cabinet had absconded, and there was no General Assembly to convene. One option would have been to set up a military governor. Frank Blair was approached to assume this dictatorial position but wisely declined. Ironically, Union adherents found an answer in the state convention that the General Assembly had created back in January. Brought into existence at Claiborne Jackson's urging and legitimized by statewide election of delegates, the convention had a sweeping charge to "consider the existing relations between the government of the United States, the people and governments of the different states, and the government and the people of the State of Missouri." This body was also granted authority to "adopt such measures for vindication of the sovereignty of the State and the protection of its institutions."

Jackson had hoped this authority would be used to carry Missouri into the Confederacy, but the "Submission Convention" had instead recommended that Missouri maintain her ties with the Union. Jackson never dreamed that, within six months, the convention would employ its authority to declare his own office and those of his cabinet vacant and proceed to create a provisional government to act hand in hand with federal authorities in suppressing rebellion within the state.

The convention's last act before adjournment in January had been to name a committee of eight with the authority to call the convention into session again before the next regularly scheduled meeting in December. On July 6, a majority of this committee voted to call the convention back into session on July 22 at Jefferson City. Of the ninety-two members originally elected, seventy-six managed to gather in Jefferson City to carry out their difficult task. A significant number of the members, some 45 percent, believed the convention did not have the constitutional authority to remove a legitimately elected government and replace it with another that had no popular mandate. On July 30, despite the deep divisions within the convention among Conditional and Unconditional Unionists, the delegates adopted the unprecedented course of declaring vacant the offices of governor, lieutenant governor, secretary of state, and all seats of the General Assembly. They repealed the military bill and other acts that the General Assembly had passed during the frantic days following Camp Jackson.

Drastic times called for drastic actions. The next day, July 31, Hamilton Gamble, who had dominated the proceedings, became the provisional governor of Missouri, and Willard P. Hall of Buchanan County was selected to fill the office of lieutenant governor. The convention instituted an oath of loyalty to the federal and provisional governments for the holders of all public offices in the state and stipulated that all voters, if and when a canvass was held, would be required to swear the oath, as well. The delegates then voted unanimously to hold a statewide election in November, at which all the actions taken by the convention would be submitted for approval by the voters. This last action alarmed Unconditional Unionists, who hardly wanted to make the question of Unionism the subject of a referendum. Missourians might reject the actions of the convention and even declare for the Confederacy. However, the voters never got that chance, for the election was later cancelled. The provisional government functioned for most of the war without seeking any electoral mandate from Missourians, loyal or otherwise.

The selection of Hamilton Gamble marked the beginning of a new era in state and federal relations. No longer would events in Missouri be controlled by the "extreme men," as Lincoln's Attorney General Edward Bates characterized Lyon, Blair, and their faction, or by the forces of Radical Republicanism, with its ranks of abolitionists and its hordes of foreign Hessians. The muscle for Lyon and Blair's astonishing success had been their army of antislavery, anti-aristocratic German citizens and immigrants. They had come to this country seeking freedom from European overlords only to encounter another class of overlords, the slaveholding Southern elites of Missouri. It was these new citizens who had done the dirty work in those crucial early months, ridding Missouri of a secessionist-leaning government and holding the state in the Union. But their services would no longer be needed if Gamble had his way. They were too extreme and too unsympathetic to the views and attitudes of a large number of Missourians who were traditionally Southern in their heritage and beliefs. Gamble would give the people a government that served the interests of wealthy slaveholders who cherished states' rights as much if not more than Unionism.

Conservatives, like Edward Bates, had won out, besting more extreme Unionists in the convention's battles. Slaveholders who dominated the political establishment believed the Union offered the best protection for slavery and chose a man who could represent their interests in Washington, D.C., as well as Missouri. Hamilton Gamble was Bates's brother-in-law, and like Frank Blair had done, exploited his family connections in the cabinet to gain direct access to Lincoln. This former Missouri lawyer and state Supreme Court justice appeared by consensus to represent the kind of leadership Missourians longed for.

The alternative was a Confederate Missouri surrounded on three sides by free states of a foreign nation that would welcome escaped slaves. The federal fugitive

Hamilton R. Gamble became provisional governor of Missouri on July 31, 1861, and served until his death on January 31, 1864. Gamble had come out of retirement to play a prominent role in the effort to keep Missouri in the Union. *Governors Portrait Gallery, Missouri State Capitol*

slave law required the return of slaves escaping to adjoining states, though the will to enforce the law did not always exist. One of Gamble's first official acts was to assure slave owners that he intended to safeguard their "peculiar institution" while preserving the Union. He also offered amnesty to followers of Jackson and Price who would lay down their arms and return to their homes. This suited Lincoln because it eased the jittery nerves of lukewarm, slave-owning Unionists in Missouri who feared that the state had fallen under the sway of radicals with scant sympathy for the Southern way of life and reckless disregard for personal property. Gamble assured such citizens that his government would not interfere with their beliefs or human property as long as they attended to peaceful pursuits.

Edward Bates of St. Louis served as Lincoln's attorney general during the Civil War. Acting in concert with his brother-in-law, Hamilton Gamble, the provisional Unionist governor, the men pursued a conservative policy aimed at protecting the interests of slaveholders in Missouri, which became the dominant policy during much of the war. *Library of Congress*

One of Gamble's first priorities was the creation of a state militia that would be under his control. He was eager to disband the Home Guards, who had been sworn into temporary Federal service by Lyon and Blair to act as a counterforce to the secessionist State Guard. They had served the purpose then, but the conservatives complained that the "foreign hirelings" were overbearing and oppressive in their treatment of Southerners. Gamble wanted to see them enlisted either in the Union army or in a state militia that he controlled. He also wanted to end the military occupation of Missouri by troops from non-slaveholding states. They tended to treat all Missourians, loyal or not, as the enemy. In this, Gamble had a valuable ally in President Lincoln, who hoped that a state militia could pacify and garrison Missouri, freeing Federal troops for service in other theaters of the war.

Gamble issued a call in late August to enlist 42,000 six-month volunteers in the Missouri militia. He received about as much response to this call as Price and Jackson had to theirs; only 6,000 men stepped forward. Gamble's timing was bad. With the military defeats at Carthage and Wilson's Creek, secessionist fortunes were on the rise while the Union ranks seemed disorganized and split by dissension.

Gamble had another serious problem, as well. He had no money to arm or equip his militia because the state treasury was empty. Gamble's response was like that of his arch rival, Claiborne Jackson. In July, Jackson journeyed to Richmond to seek funds and military aid from Jefferson Davis. In a face-to-face meeting, Davis overcame his distrust of Jackson and provided funds and military aid. Now Gamble, at the end of August, was in Washington in search of similar aid from Abraham Lincoln. He, too, was successful, getting a presidential promise of arms and a two-hundred-thousand-dollar loan. The president also instructed the newly appointed commander of the

Department of the West to cooperate fully with Gamble's government.

This commander was Maj. Gen. John C. Frémont, who had taken up his position around the same time that Gamble became provisional governor. Frémont vigorously opposed Gamble's plan for an independent state militia in late July. He shared Lyon's view that state leaders had no constitutional authority to interfere with the conduct of federal military operations within Missouri, nor should they have any control of such operations. He urged Lincoln to give no authority to Gamble to raise regiments in Missouri. Unfortunately for Frémont, he had managed to alienate most of his potential allies, including Frank Blair, who might have otherwise supported him in this struggle against Bates and Gamble.

Frémont had left Lyon unsupported at Wilson's Creek but might have survived the fiasco had he not excluded Blair and leading St. Louis Unionists from his inner circle. He established himself in splendid isolation at his lavish headquarters in the Brant Mansion in St. Louis. He made matters worse by surrounding himself with an outsized staff of European revolutionaries and mercenaries and a personal bodyguard of 150 cavalry, unauthorized by the federal government but decked out in plumed hats and blue uniforms with all the trimmings. St. Louis and Missouri leaders wishing to confer with the department commander had to get past his "viceregal court—the main requirement for which seemed to be inability to speak English."

Once while attempting to gain admission to meet with Frémont, the governor was kept waiting for an hour before leaving in complete disgust. It is little wonder that Gamble joined the growing ranks calling for Frémont's removal. Frémont's supercilious behavior drove off allies that he desperately needed. The most prominent defector was Frank Blair, who now became an odd bedfellow with Hamilton Gamble in a campaign to rid Missouri of Frémont's seemingly ineffective leadership. Without allies to back him in his struggle with Gamble and Blair, the commanding general got no support from the Lincoln administration to derail formation of a state militia.

This did not mean that Frémont was going to cooperate with Gamble or provide him arms for his militia. In truth he had no arms to give, for the vast industrial capacity of the United States had not yet geared up to produce weapons in great numbers. Everyone scrounged for arms. Since Frémont had none to spare, Gamble received authorization from Lincoln to procure four thousand arms from federal armories, but something less than three thousand Garibaldi rifles and other foreign weapons could actually be located by his agent.

Gamble made little headway in his negotiations with Frémont, nor did the Pathfinder wrench many concessions from Gamble. Frémont wanted to appoint brigadiers of his choosing to the militia, but Gamble told him that Frémont had no powers to effect this because, under the existing law, the militia elected its own officers. But Frémont still held a tenuous lease on his command, and he moved boldly to his next blunder, the declaration of martial law.

There were unclear legal precedents and no Congressional authorization for local military authorities to declare a state of martial law or to suspend the writ of habeas corpus. However, Lincoln allowed his commanders to exercise their own discretion to invoke martial law and suspend habeas corpus if they believed it was militarily necessary to establish control in areas of insurrection where normal legal and governmental apparatus no longer functioned. Frémont availed himself of this authority almost immediately upon his arrival to St. Louis in early August and placed the entire city under martial law. Soon, he began to close down pro-Southern presses, as well as loyal newspapers critical of his administration. Outspoken

Maj. Gen. John C. Frémont, the famous Pathfinder of the West and first Republican presidential candidate, seemed the perfect man to manage military affairs in Missouri. Unfortunately, Frémont developed a knack for making enemies and presided over a series of military reverses that undid much of what Frank Blair and Nathaniel Lyon had accomplished in the opening months of the war. Within one hundred days, the Pathfinder would be gone. *Used by permission, State Historical Society of Missouri, Columbia*

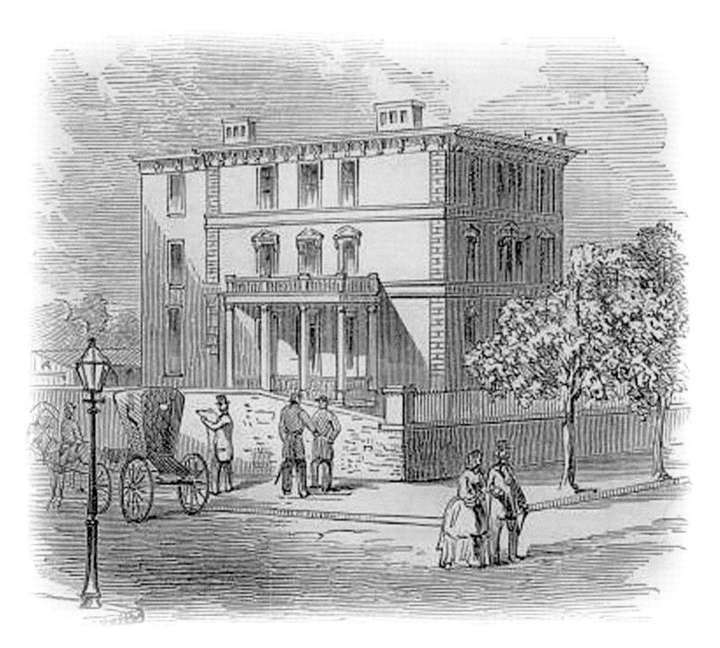

Gen. John C. Frémont established his headquarters in the Brant Mansion in St. Louis when he assumed command of the western department in the summer of 1861. Critics accused Frémont of living in palatial splendor, pointing out the extravagant six-thousand-dollar annual rent of his quarters. *Harper's Weekly*

Southern men found themselves under arrest by Frémont's foreign guards, who tramped through the streets seeking out citizens who weeks before had defiantly displayed Confederate flags from their windows.

On August 30, the general extended martial law to encompass a large portion of the state. If Gamble hoped to pacify out-state Missouri by replacing Federal troops with a state militia, by granting amnesty to ex-Guardsmen, and by restoring the authority of local governments and civil courts, Frémont represented the opposite tack. He shared the view of the Unconditional Unionist faction in St. Louis that a strong Federal presence was required in the state because a large proportion of the population was sympathetic to the Southern cause. Not only that, the Southern sympathizers gave aid and comfort to the enemy, especially to bands of guerrillas who were starting to become active in several sections of Missouri.

In his proclamation of martial law, Frémont stated that property was being devastated by bands of murderers and marauders and that life itself had become insecure. The daily increase of crime and outrages was driving inhabitants away and

All persons found in arms north of a line extending from Cape Girardeau and Ironton through Rolla and Jefferson City to Leavenworth, Kansas, would be court-martialed and, if convicted, executed. Anyone who had taken up arms or actively assisted enemies in the field would have their property confiscated and their slaves set free.

ruining the state. Missouri was helpless, making it necessary for Frémont to assume administrative powers of the state by proclaiming martial law throughout Missouri. All persons found in arms north of a line extending from Cape Girardeau and Ironton through Rolla and Jefferson City to Leavenworth, Kansas, would be court-martialed and, if convicted, executed. Anyone who had taken up arms or actively assisted enemies in the field would have their property confiscated and their slaves set free.

Frémont was in way over his head when he took these steps. Instantly, he caught everyone's attention, including Lincoln's. The president rightly feared that proposed executions would inflame the North-South conflict to a war of mutual extermination. The South would naturally respond in kind, and indeed, M. Jeff Thompson thundered from the swamps of southeast Missouri, "For every member of the Missouri State Guard, or soldier of our allies the Confederate states, who shall be put to death in pursuance of said order of General Frémont, I will *hang*, *draw*, and *quarter* a minion of said Abraham Lincoln."

The president promptly countermanded that portion of Frémont's proclamation—no one would be shot without Lincoln's personal approval. As for freeing slaves of opponents, Lincoln spelled out to Frémont the potentially disastrous consequences of this action: "This will alarm our Southern Union friends, and turn them against us—perhaps ruin our rather fair prospect for Kentucky." Historian Bruce Catton explained the implications of Frémont's proposals: They would commit the states of the Union and Confederacy "to an entirely different kind of war; a remorseless revolutionary struggle, which in the end could do nothing less than redefine the very nature of the American experiment, committing the American people for the rest of time to a much broader concept of the quality and meaning of freedom and democracy than anything they had yet embraced." It would take many more bloody battles to elevate the war to this level. Missouri would lag back and cling to slavery to the last possible moment.

When Frémont refused to rescind this part of the proclamation voluntarily, Lincoln "very cheerfully" did so. Only two slaves managed to gain their freedom under Frémont's proclamation; they had belonged to Thomas L. Snead but had escaped into Union lines. Frémont made matters worse by dispatching his wife, Jesse, the spirited and high-tempered daughter of Missouri Sen. Thomas Hart Benton, to meet with Lincoln. The president gave her a chilly reception and claimed that "she more than once intimated that if General Frémont should decide to try conclusions with me, he could set up for himself." If the goal had been to lose Lincoln's confidence, Frémont succeeded. Jesse also met with Francis Preston Blair, Sr., and managed to alienate this long-standing friend and protector. The Frémonts had broken with the family who had helped make their rise to power possible and who would soon help to orchestrate their fall.

Frémont's proclamation did receive an enthusiastic reception in Radical Republican circles. Many in the St. Louis German community warmly embraced the revolutionary measures and transferred their allegiance from Frank Blair to Frémont. Although Frank Blair approved of the emancipation feature of the proclamation, he approved of little else and drifted toward the conservative wing of the Republican party. Meanwhile the leadership of the Unconditional Union men, including a large faction of the Germans, fell to B. Gratz Brown. This group preferred immediate and uncompensated emancipation, while Blair favored gradual emancipation of slaves in stages. The formerly solid German block was now dividing into Frémont and Blair factions and losing much of its clout in the process.

One feature of Frémont's proclamation did stick; martial law would continue to be applied to Missouri by his successors. The local courts would exercise civil authority in pacified areas, but in guerrilla-infested locales or in areas reduced to chaos by contesting armies, martial law was the only law in effect.

CHAPTER 6

Choosing Sides North Missouri Style

$\mathcal{E}$ VENTS IN NORTHEAST MISSOURI in July 1861 provided a foretaste of the coming guerrilla war and the effects it would have on civilians, soldiers, and partisans. Secessionist nightriders in bands of varying sizes roamed the rolling hills of the hinterlands north and west of St. Louis all the way to the Iowa line. They began wreaking havoc along the Hannibal and St. Joseph and north Missouri railroads, burning bridges, tearing out culverts, and firing into troop trains. One of the more dramatic incidents occurred on July 10, when a group of 300 to 400 men attacked the Hannibal and St. Joseph Railroad at Monroe Station (today's Monroe City) and burned the railroad depot, outbuildings, and seventeen passenger and freight cars.

An energetic, West Point-trained brigadier general from Illinois, John Pope, drew the assignment of bringing the situation under control. Like many other Free State officers who rode into the Missouri backcountry, he discovered an unsettled social and political terrain where a tangled web of conflicting loyalties divided neighborhoods and even families. Pope found a chaotic situation in which bands of twenty to thirty lawless men wandered the countryside committing depredations at will. Pope certainly didn't credit these hit-and-run raiders as military forces of the enemy operating inside Federal lines. Rather, he considered these men, most of whom were probably Missouri State Guard partisans, as mere criminals undeserving of mercy. Establishing drastic countermeasures later formalized by department commanders Frémont and Henry Halleck, Pope decreed that such marauders actually captured in acts of sabotage would be court-martialed and executed.

The local folk seemed to Pope either in complete sympathy with the Southern cause, or if Union-minded, to look the other way when their neighbors committed unlawful acts. According to Pope, Unionists "even most opposed to [the marauders']

John Pope's Civil War career began in Missouri, where he had responsibility for clearing out guerrillas in north Missouri. *Library of Congress*

Reenactment photo, Department of Natural Resources (top)

lawless conduct would carefully shield them from exposure." The locals invariably seemed willfully unhelpful if not downright hostile in their dealings with soldiers who were invading their neighborhoods from neighboring Yankee states. Pope encountered what became the standard state of affairs in Missouri's rural areas—the local population that the Union army allegedly protected seemed in most instances to be giving aid and comfort to the enemy. "The mass of the people stood quietly looking on at a few men in their midst committing all sorts of atrocious acts, and neither attempted to prevent them nor to give any information by which they could have been prevented and punished." Pope applied this characterization equally to every inhabitant of the region, no matter their true political leanings. "No surprises," he said, "are possible in a country where *all* the inhabitants are willing to warn, if not to assist," guerrillas.

The circumstances made every anti-guerrilla operation not only dangerous but also profoundly frustrating for Federal patrols. Without cooperation from local citizens, the task of exterminating guerrillas became vastly more difficult. "When troops were sent out against these marauders, they found only men quietly working in the field or sitting in their offices, who as soon as the backs of the Federal soldiers were turned, were again in arms and menacing the peace."

Loyal Unionists in the district were too timid to stand against or even provide information about the Rebel bands, thus making them little better than their secessionist neighbors, in Pope's mind. These lukewarm loyalists might have been won to the Federal side had they not ended up on Pope's "enemies" list along with practically everyone else in northeast Missouri. Pope believed the partisan war "can only be ended by making all engaged in it suffer for every act of hostility committed." Even at this early stage of the war, Union authorities like Pope had begun to experiment with the tactics of total warfare later epitomized by Gen. William T. Sherman's march through Georgia and South Carolina to the sea. In loyal Missouri, as much as in any of the rebellious Confederate states, the entire civilian populace came to feel the "hard hand of war."

Pope's imperfectly formed evaluation of the loyalty of his district led him to lower the hammer of Federal harshness on the amorphous civilian population rather than on the palpable enemy before him, the organized bands of nightriders and marauders. He commanded more than 2,000 soldiers. Those troops might have been sent out in combat patrols, carrying the war to the partisans in their own neighborhoods, but Pope knew this method of guerrilla fighting would be tough and brutal. "This course would have led to frequent and bloody encounters, to searching of houses, and arrests in many cases of innocent persons."

Soon all of the above tactics would be liberally applied in the statewide anti-guerrilla effort, but at this time, Pope instead decided to subject the entire citizenry under his control to a gigantic experiment to modify human behavior through the use of negative stimuli. Pope expected civilians to control the lawlessness in their own neighborhoods or forfeit their property to pay for damages to railroad bridges and the like as punishment for their failure to prevent such acts from happening: "Union men and secessionists would alike engage in putting a stop to lawless and predatory bands, and ... the persons themselves who had joined these armed marauders would soon cease their forays and abandon their organizations when they discovered that ... every act they committed hostile to the peace of the country was a blow not only at their own property and safety, but also at that of their own friends and relatives." Pope hoped to eliminate partisan warfare without actually having to fight any partisans.

Pope soon dispatched officers and troops to the major towns in his district with orders to establish committees of public safety. These committees were to be made up of the most prominent Union and Southern men of the towns—men of substance and respectability—but with the majority composed of gentlemen of "secessionist proclivities." Pope was convinced that "when once the secessionists are made to understand that upon peace in their midst depends the safety of their families and property, we shall soon have quiet again in North Missouri."

By the end of August, Pope could proudly report to his superior, Maj. Gen. John Charles Frémont, that his policy alone and the fear of the penalties to property prescribed in it had prevented the secessionists from driving out Union men and destroying property. He went on, "The secession papers in North Missouri are now entreating the population to preserve the peace, because the leading State-rights men (secessionists) are made to serve on committees of safety against their will, and their property is made responsible for any violence or breach of peace committed by their friends." He claimed that had he fought the guerrillas with conventional military force, he would have needed five times the number of troops required by his punitive offensive directed against civilians.

There was one exception to this rosy generalization. In Marion County, an unknown group of gunmen fired into a train full of troops, provoking Pope to send 600 Illinois troops with two pieces of artillery to occupy Marion County. These troops were commanded by an Illinois lawyer and politician named Stephen A. Hurlbut, who had parlayed his friendship with Lincoln into a general's star. Pope required that the residents of the county furnish quarters, subsistence, and transportation to Hurlbut's men as a result of their failure to control the attacks on the railroad. A deputation of citizens begged to have the levy against them lifted, and Pope relented briefly. But their amnesty proved short-lived when, Pope noted, "the troops, which had been quartered at Palmyra, had not proceeded three miles from the place before the train carrying them was fired into from the roadside, and one man killed and several wounded."

Stephen A. Hurlbut gained his brigadier general's star through political connections but went on to become a corps commander in Sherman's army. His performance in Missouri was less stellar. During the summer of 1861, he unleashed his 600 untrained Illinois troops on the helpless civilian population of Marion County. *Library of Congress*

Once again the hammer of retribution landed on the hapless population. Pope was well aware that the out-of-state troops sent to Marion County to enforce his harsh codes were hardly seasoned soldiers. There had been no time to set up a camp of instruction to instill habits of discipline and efficiency in his men; they were still green. Pope knew that "raw troops such as these grow worse every day by this system of small detachments scattered over the country on police duty, and if it be pursued for two months, I shall have a mob and not an army to command." It didn't take two months for these undisciplined troops to wreak havoc in Marion County; it happened almost immediately upon their arrival. The soldiers had been sent in to protect the Hannibal and St. Joseph Railroad, but their actions had the opposite effect of placing the rail line in even greater danger of attack. This was the consequence of a policy that failed to distinguish between friend and foe and that punished the loyal and disloyal alike. The unfortunate result of such a policy was to transform natural allies into bitter opponents.

Soon the loudest critic of Pope's policy became J. T. Hayward, the general manager of the Hannibal and St. Joseph Railroad, the very line that Pope was supposed to be protecting. He joined a rising chorus of protestors against the outrageous treatment being meted out by Pope's "mob" of soldiers. He ably represented the citizens' version of what was happening in Marion County. For one thing, Hayward believed, the men, who fired on the trains, were probably outsiders,

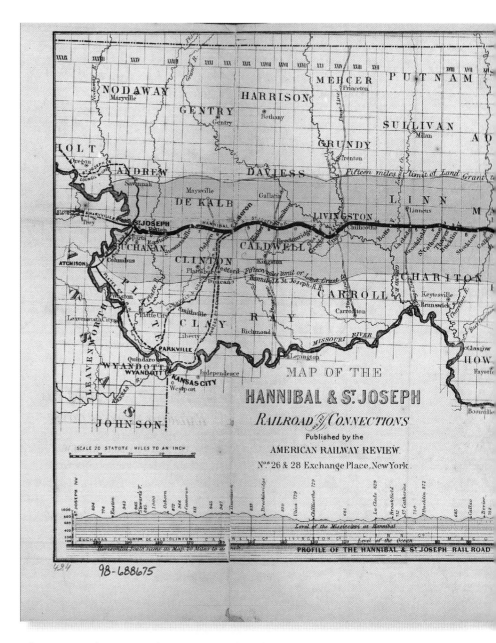

who were unknown in the area. He also claimed that all citizens of the county, no matter what their political beliefs, deplored the violence perpetrated by these strangers.

Hayward's remonstrance did not keep Federal troops from descending on Palmyra with a vengeance, and they threatened to stay until local leaders delivered the men guilty of firing on the train. While they stayed, the troops were to be quartered and provisioned by the residents. When the county court and city failed to come up with rations or funds for expenses, a company of Illinois soldiers helped themselves to the goods of several stores. The local hotel keeper, a Union man, got nothing for feeding the troops: "One thousand dollars will not make me whole, and if it goes on much longer, I am ruined." Pope's men entered and searched private residences and, in the searing summer sun, compelled leading citizens to perform forced labor such as digging trenches. The troops stole everything that wasn't bolted down or secreted away, including pigs, poultry, milk, butter, preserves, potatoes, horses, and anything else they wanted. One trainload of departing troops heading back to

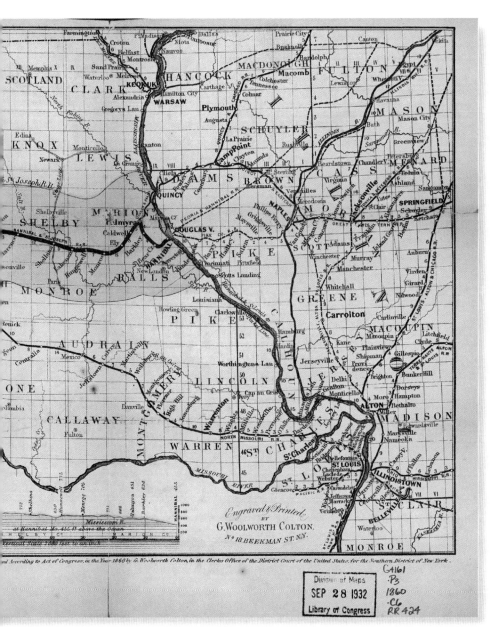

In 1859, the Hannibal and St. Joseph Railroad became the first rail line to be completed across the state from the Mississippi River to the Missouri River. The North Missouri Railroad, completed a few months later, connected the Hannibal and St. Joseph with St. Louis. Gen. John Pope was dispatched to protect the strategically important rail line from marauding bands of guerrillas. *Map of the Hannibal and St. Joseph Railroad and Its Connections, 1860. Library of Congress*

Illinois also carried more than sixty horses and mules commandeered from Marion County, as well as several slaves. Some soldiers got drunk, raped female slaves, and fired on civilians from passing trains, all with complete impunity. According to Hayward, "If the thing goes on this way much longer … I fear we cannot run the road or live in the country except under military protection. It is enough to drive a people to madness, and it is doing it fast."

Pope admitted that his policy might turn some lukewarm Union men toward secession, but he believed more firmly that without his policy "thousands of good Union men would have been driven from their homes and their property despoiled." However, the driving out and despoiling were being done by his Federal soldiers, not the guerrillas. Hayward, who knew the local situation, saw circumstances quite differently than Pope: "The effect has been to make a great many Union men inveterate enemies, and if these things continue much longer, our cause is ruined." The misery lasted another month. By mid-September, both the secessionists and Pope were gone, the former to join Price, the latter to St. Joseph.

Martin E. Green was a county judge, farmer, sawmill owner, and Breckinridge Democrat. Local Southern sympathizers responded in large numbers to his call to join the State Guard. His inability to defeat David Moore's Home Guards at the Battle of Athens left north Missouri in Union hands. *Missouri Department of Natural Resources*

The real battle for control of northeast Missouri took place on the northern fringe of Pope's district, in Clark County. Here, at the town of Athens, along the banks of the Des Moines River, Missouri's northernmost Civil War battle was fought on August 5, five days before the bloody encounter at Wilson's Creek. Pope thought that for the folk of this region, the outbreak of civil war was little more than an excuse to kick their local feuds up to a higher level of violence: "It is to be borne in mind that the disturbances in North Missouri are purely local and personal, and have no view to the result of the great operations of Government. The people in that region are merely fighting with each other, in many cases to satisfy feelings of personal hostility of long standing." Pope's analysis as it applied to the Battle of Athens was only partially correct—to the extent that the scrap at Athens truly was a neighbor-against-neighbor affair. But if he thought that the Missourians of this area were not as passionate and opinionated about the all-consuming political issues of the day as anyone else, Pope badly underestimated their convictions.

Although there were few slaves in this area, there were plenty of Southern sympathizers. According to a local saying, "Secesh" were easily generated from brush country and bad whiskey. Local Southern men responded in large numbers to the call to enroll in the State Guard. The summons came from Martin E. Green, a local county court judge, farmer, sawmill owner, and true-hearted Breckinridge Democrat whose brother, James S. Green, had been until recently a pro-South U.S. senator. The volunteers assembled at a place called Horseshoe Bend on the Fabius River in Lewis County and elected Martin Green as their colonel. For second in command, they selected a prominent farmer from Knox County named Joseph C. Porter. Both Martin and Porter were capable leaders and deeply devoted to the Southern cause. Both left their marks on the Civil War landscape in the months ahead and ultimately gave their lives for the Southern cause.

There were few men with military experience in the State Guard camp. Consequently, the new recruits received little by way of drill or instruction. They had no proper weapons but instead brought their trusty fowling pieces and squirrel rifles. They were eager to sight these guns not on wild game but on their Unionist neighbors, whom they hoped to drive from northeast Missouri. There were even rumors that the secessionists might cross the Des Moines River, invade Iowa, and attack Croton, a notorious station on the Underground Railroad.

The local Unionists may well have been imbibing some of the local moonshine as well, for their blood was up, and they were spoiling to mix it up with their Southern-leaning neighbors: "Secessionists and Rebel traitors desiring a fight can be accommodated on demand," a recruiting placard read. For their leader, the Unionists picked David Moore, a Clark County merchant and Douglas Democrat who, according to a contemporary, "could get madder and swear longer without repeating himself than any man I ever knew." He had served in the Mexican War, which gave him a leg up in military experience over his enemies. The fault line of loyalties ran right through the middle of the Moore family. His wife was a secessionist who freely spoke her mind. Two of his sons went off to find Green's Horseshoe Bend camp and join the Confederate-sympathizing State Guard, while a third son would shortly enter Confederate service.

Most of the Union men of Clark County came forward to join the Home Guard regiment being formed. There was no safety for loyal men in remaining home alone in what were becoming mean neighborhoods where a gang of State Guard horsemen might come riding down the lane unexpectedly at any moment. Frémont had sent .58 caliber ammunition and Springfield rifles to arm the Home Guards along the northern border. Moore managed to lay his hands on two hundred of the rifles, and he received additional military muskets. In late July, Moore set up headquarters in Athens, a prosperous town of perhaps a thousand people situated on the banks of the Des Moines River opposite the hamlet of Croton, Iowa. At Athens, Moore was just across the river from reinforcements, supplies, and weapons from the Free State stronghold of Iowa.

Tensions in the region were high. At the beginning of July, a Southern man in Canton shot and killed a Home Guard captain, which triggered an exchange of gunfire between men of both sides. Three weeks later, Moore launched a raid on Etna in Scotland County, scattered a few State Guard defenders, and pulled down a flagpole that flew a State Guard flag. This time a Southern sympathizer lost his life. Meanwhile, Col. Martin Green was in motion as well, riding west and north with his State Guardsmen, sweeping small Home Guard detachments before him and entering towns to the cheers and adulation of local secessionist folk. Green continued toward Athens, which he needed to clear of Unionists before he headed south to link up with Price. Otherwise the vacated region would be left firmly in Federal control, with Southern-leaning residents facing persecution.

Citizens of Athens knew Green was bearing down on their town and dreaded the prospect of a pitched battle. They gathered at community leader Joseph Benning's house and pleaded with Colonel Moore not to bring on a fight. In his usual blunt manner, Moore roundly rejected any talk of capitulation or retreat and declared, "If Mart Green desires to avoid the shedding of blood, he had better keep his men beyond the range of my muskets!" As Green approached with a host rumored to number 4,000 men, Moore called on Keokuk, Iowa, for reinforcements. But many Iowans had some reason or another for not hastening to Moore's aid, and most failed to show up in time for the battle. Someone accused them of developing a sudden case of "states' rights." To make matters worse, a number of Moore's Clark County recruits were absent on leave and did not appear for the stand against the secessionists. In the ensuing rough-and-tumble battle, it would be Missourians spilling the blood of fellow Missourians; the antagonists would often be neighbors who personally knew each other.

On the evening of August 4, Green and his host were camped at the village of Chambersburg, six miles southwest of Athens. Long before sunrise the next day, they were on the move. Moore learned that the enemy was headed his way and ordered his men to sleep on their arms. Before dawn on August 5, Moore formed 333 of his men along Spring Street in Athens and prepared to give battle. By first light, Green's Guardsmen could be made out moving through the woods and brush on the edges of town. The precise size of Green's force is unknown but has been estimated to have been closer to between 1,000 and 2,000 men. Whatever the real number, there is no doubt that Colonel Moore, with only 400 to 500 men, was greatly outnumbered. To make matters worse, Green had three artillery pieces: a nine-pounder, six-pounder, and a homemade cannon fashioned from a hollow log.

Moore had no artillery but did possess two advantages over Green. First, his men had received some training, while Green's men were little more than an undisciplined mob. Second, he had superior military weapons, including Springfield rifles and plenty of ammunition. Green's men, if they had arms at all, carried their personal hunting pieces. Green may have hoped that the smaller Union force would flee rather than give battle. If so, he sorely underestimated the mettle of David Moore and his followers.

As Green neared Athens, he sent detachments of men to take up positions along the creeks, ravines, and fields and flank the east and west sides of Athens. Green and the larger part of his force moved along the main road and entered the town

David Moore was a Clark County merchant and Douglas Democrat who could actually boast some military experience—he had fought in the Mexican War. He commanded a Union Home Guard regiment in northeast Missouri and won an important victory over secessionists at the Battle of Athens on August 5, 1861. *Missouri Department of Natural Resources*

Joseph Benning's house in Athens was a target, inadvertent or otherwise, in the shelling of the town by State Guard forces under Martin Green. Capt. J.W. Kneisley's artillery battery, inexperienced, fired wildly and a cannonball passed through the front and back sides of Benning's house, now a part of the Battle of Athens State Historic Site. The damage is still visible.
James M. Denny, Missouri Department of Natural Resources

from the south. At the brow of a hill overlooking the Home Guard position, he deployed his artillery battery in the center and arrayed his men in line of battle on either side. Three hundred yards ahead stood Moore's small force, its back to the Des Moines River and surrounded by the enemy on the other three sides. To deal with the enemy massed on his western flank, Moore dispatched 60 men to confront the State Guardsmen formed along Stallion Branch. On the eastern flank, a force of Green's men under Maj. Ben Shacklett had taken up position in a cornfield next to the river. Moore sent his second in command, Lt. Col. Charles Callihan, a washed-out West Pointer turned preacher, to deal with Shacklett's men. To accomplish this mission, Callihan had an infantry company under Capt. Elsbury Small and a cavalry unit of Clark Countians.

The battle began at 5:30 a.m., when Green's artillery battery, commanded by Capt. J. W. Kneisley, opened fire. Later in the war, this battery would acquire a deadly reputation, but this was their first action. They had not yet learned how to aim their pieces. Most of the few cannonballs they fired sailed wildly over the Des Moines River and crashed into Croton, bringing the Civil War to Iowa soil. One cannonball passed completely through Joseph Benning's house in Athens, and the entrance and exit holes can be seen to this day. The hollow log cannon, meanwhile, exploded the first time it was fired and injured its attendants.

Men on both sides began to unleash the first shots that most of them had ever fired in anger. Soon the crack of rifles could be heard across the opposing lines of battle. Gradually, Green's men started to advance toward the line of Home Guards, who in turn fired volley after volley with their new Springfield rifles. On the west flank, Home Guardsmen under Captains Barton Hackney and John Cox held their own against the more numerous Southern forces led by H.J. Dull and a man named Kimbrough. On the east side of the battlefield, Shacklett and his men pushed through the cornfield toward Callihan's forces. Seeing that he was outnumbered, the "fighting parson" Callihan turned tail and fled with his command across the Des Moines River, followed by the frightened horsemen from Clark County. This left Captain Small (at 350 pounds, inappropriately named) and his lone company to face Shacklett's advancing Guardsmen. Small proved to be a fighter as he and his men stood their ground in the face of the larger State Guard force.

All across the line, the superior range and accuracy of the Union rifles began to take their toll on the attackers, and casualties began to mount. According to one account of the battle, "The Rebels seemed quite disconcerted at their rough reception. Their first onset was met and withstood. The rapid volleys from their shotguns and rifles were answered by the steady fire of the Federal muskets, and there was no indication that the Unionists were disposed to fly the field. Blood began to flow, men fell dead, and wounded comrades reeled and staggered."

As a result, Green's assault began to waver, and Moore sensed that the time had come to unleash a charge. His stentorian voice could be heard across the Union line bellowing, "Forward! Charge bayonets!" One legend states that Moore's son in the secessionist ranks exclaimed, "The old man's mad, fellers; I'm going home." As Moore's charge bore down on Green's inexperienced and untrained Guardsmen, their nerve failed in the face of the bayonets of the advancing Home Guards.

Green attempted to rally his men, but it was too late. They broke for the rear and fled in wild disorder. On the eastern flank, Shacklett received a serious wound in the neck and lost control of his men, who joined the headlong flight. Only Dull and Kimbrough on the west side of the battlefield proved able to conduct an orderly retreat. Kneisley managed to get his artillery battery limbered in time to join the stampede. One chronicler stated, "A wild and almost inexplicable panic seized upon the little secession army. It was a miniature Bull Run. In their frantic rush for the rear, scores of men did not stop to mount their horses, but pushed on afoot." Moore's victorious Home Guards pursued the retreating secessionists for a mile before turning back to collect the spoils abandoned by the panic-stricken foe. They gathered 450 horses, saddles, and bridles, hundreds of discarded weapons, and a wagonload of knives that were supposed to have been used to carve up Yankees.

The Battle of Athens took less than two hours from start to finish. There was little loss of life. Three were killed and 20 wounded on the Federal side, while Moore estimated Green's loss at 31 killed and wounded. Although this battle, like that fought at Boonville back in June, was a small affair by almost any standard, it nonetheless determined who would control northeast Missouri. For the remainder of the war, this region would remain in the Union column.

Athens was not the last time that Green and Moore and their men fought each other. A little more than a year later, in October 1862, the two commanders squared off again at the Battle of Corinth, Mississippi. By then, the Home Guards who had fought at Athens had been organized into the Twenty-First Missouri Infantry. Prior to Corinth, the regiment fought in the bloody Battle of Shiloh. Moore sustained three wounds there that ultimately cost him his right leg. Before the war ended, his Twenty-First Missouri would lose 309 men.

Green's men went on to fight at Lexington, and many enrolled in the Missouri Confederate Brigade the following December. In that brigade, they participated in some of the bloodiest battles of the Civil War: Pea Ridge, Vicksburg, Atlanta, Franklin, and many others. No brigade fought more bravely or lost more men in the service of the Lost Cause than the storied Missouri Confederate Brigade.

Both Moore and Green earned brigadier general stars. Green was killed on the ramparts of Vicksburg, but Moore survived the war and returned to northeast Missouri. Such soldiers and such leaders had long since proved wrong Pope's sneer that northeast Missouri men were motivated by local rivalries rather than deeply held convictions.

Following the Athens debacle, Martin Green and his men remained in northeast Missouri for another six weeks. Pope dispatched General Hurlbut to run him to ground, but Green and his men took advantage of a network of local informants and had little difficulty eluding their pursuers. The most significant encounter with Green's command came in early September at Shelbina. Here Green managed to surround a regiment of the Second Kansas Infantry and a detachment of the Third Iowa Infantry under the command of Col. N. G. Williams. Using his two cannons, Green pinned down the Federals in Shelbina while his men pulled up railroad tracks on either side of the town. Williams wanted to counterattack and attempt to seize the State Guard artillery, but the officers of the Second Kansas refused to give battle, claiming that the enlistments of their men were up and they were in no mood to fight. The Kansans had been among the worst looters and drunkards in northeast Missouri. In a belated attempt to restore discipline in his district, Pope arrested the Kansas commander, along with two officers of the Sixteenth Illinois Infantry.

David Moore played a role in the pursuit of Green. In mid-September, he attacked a party of 50 men, presumably from Green's command, killed two of them, and dispersed the rest. By then Frémont had decided it was time to get tough: "I have resolved upon a combined attack on Green's men and their total annihilation." He ordered Pope to concentrate his forces and attack the Guardsmen. But he was too late. By the time Pope could mount his forces, Green's mounted infantry was already heading out of the region. On September 14, Frémont received a dispatch that Green and 1,200 men had arrived at Glasgow, commandeered a steamer, and crossed the Missouri River. They were on their way to join Sterling Price at Lexington.

CHAPTER 7

High Tide for the Missouri Southern Cause

THE UNION ARMY largely abandoned western Missouri after Wilson's Creek, opening a wide gateway of invasion northward all the way to the banks of the Missouri River. Maj. Gen. Sterling Price had every intention of taking advantage of the opportunity as it developed. He envisioned a grand scheme to undo the previous disasters suffered by his forces in which the State Guard would return triumphantly to the state's heartland along the Missouri River. Tens of thousands of new recruits would join him there, and with this steadfast army, Price would capture Jefferson City and St. Louis, regaining control of the state and nullifying the victories of Blair, the late Lyon, and their legions of foreign-born mercenaries. Missouri's secession and assumption of her rightful place in the galaxy of the Confederacy would follow. A new fighting front would be opened that would relieve pressure on beleaguered Confederate forces elsewhere.

This strategic vision guided Price from the first months of the war to its bitter end four years later. However, as he was wont to do, the general overestimated the magnitude of the opportunity as well as the resources of the Confederacy. He and the Missouri soldiers and politicians were the lone visionaries.

Beginning with President Jefferson Davis, there was little enthusiasm in the Confederate high command for Price's master strategy of prosecuting the war in the West and scant interest in opening a front in Missouri at all. The state had yet to join the Confederacy officially, and Southern commanders were more concerned with holding positions along the Mississippi River. Generals Leonidas Polk, Gideon Pillow, and William Hardee discussed a combined assault on St. Louis through southeastern Missouri. Jeff Thompson was ever eager to lead the charge, but the generals could not form a unified plan of action that overcame severe shortages of men and material. Confederate military presence in Missouri barely extended beyond tenuous footholds at New Madrid and Springfield.

The Battle of Lexington revealed serious ineptitude on the part of the Union high command. Frémont had allowed Sterling Price to march his State Guard to the Missouri River heartland, besiege the Union garrison at Lexington, subdue it at leisure, and linger an additional ten days before an army could be organized to march against him. *Used by permission, State Historical Society of Missouri, Columbia*

Sterling Price garnered his greatest triumph at Lexington, and the battle was purely a Missouri State Guard victory. *Missouri Department of Natural Resources, Battle of Lexington State Historic Site*

The impasse between Confederate commanders in the east was nothing compared to the enmity that had developed between Price and Gen. Ben McCulloch. The two men would barely speak to each other after Wilson's Creek, let alone cooperate on any proposed offensive into Missouri. After the battle, McCulloch freely expressed his disgust with his Missouri allies, writing to his superiors and to President Davis that Price's army was no more than an armed mob. The disaffected Texan complained that the perpetually improvident Missourians pilfered unguarded tents and clothes from better-equipped Confederate forces, refused to return weapons loaned to them, and scavenged arms from dead and wounded Arkansawyers on the battlefield. He also bemoaned that Price wrongly claimed credit for the capture of Sigel's artillery by McCulloch's men. When the Missourians finally gave up the five guns, they were missing the horses and harness to pull them. Still worse, they would not share intelligence, and they fled under fire. Price's undisciplined Missourians, McCulloch claimed, were a bad influence on his own troops.

As a former Texas Ranger and Indian fighter, McCulloch should have had a better feel for the Missouri soldiers. Had he been inclined to give credit where it was due, McCulloch might have also mentioned that Price and his Missourians fought the hardest at Wilson's Creek, standing their ground despite high casualties. But McCulloch, who aspired to be a grand commander of Regular armies himself, simply could no longer stand Price. He found the Missouri general overbearing and patronizing. He refused to recognize any military ability in him or his subordinates. Demonstrating his disregard for the political realities facing Price and the Missourians, McCulloch complained that the State Guard officers were mere politicians posing as military men. The tension between the Confederate and Missouri armies was so palpable, the Texan claimed, that he "had as well be in Boston." After lingering for two weeks in Springfield, McCulloch sent General Pearce's Arkansawyers back to Bentonville, Arkansas, took his Louisiana and Texas troops south to Fayetteville, and spent the rest of the campaigning season complaining about the Missourians.

The dissension between the Southern generals squandered their real fighting chance in Missouri. Federal strategy was in disarray in the aftermath of Wilson's Creek, and secessionist fortunes rose as news of the victory spread. There had never been a better opportunity for the state's redemption, but Price was the only Southern strategist prepared to act. He turned his army north toward the Missouri heartland and the best prospect of ridding Missouri of the yoke of Federal domination. But Price and the Missouri State Guard would fight on their own hook; the Confederacy offered nothing at this critical moment. When Price and McCulloch met again in 1862, the Missouri State Guard, entirely dispossessed from its home state, was residing in Arkansas.

Price wasted little time, sending Gen. James S. Rains's cavalry ahead to scout for Kansas forces in the vicinity of Fort Scott, Kansas. The main army followed on August 26, leaving Springfield in a northwesterly direction toward Fort Scott. By the last day of August, Price and about 6,000 men encamped three miles west of Nevada. Three hundred recruits from Pike County were expected to arrive at any time.

On September 2 at Dry Wood Creek, about six miles east of the Kansas border, Price's advance under Brig. Gen. A. E. Steen encountered a force of 800 Kansas volunteers led by James H. Lane, the *bête noire* of the Missouri-Kansas border. The fire-breathing abolitionist played a dual role at Dry Creek as a U.S. senator from Kansas and a brigadier general of volunteers. Kansas had already formed two good infantry regiments, but they had been shot to pieces with Lyon at Wilson's Creek and retreated to Rolla. The Kansas border would have been largely undefended but for Lane's vigorous and entirely unauthorized recruiting. He hastily cobbled together a scratch force around Fort Scott after Wilson's Creek, including many southwestern Missouri Unionists who had fled to Kansas rather than Rolla. Their alternative had been to remain at home until hunted down by the bands of secessionists patrolling the countryside in the weeks following Lyon's defeat.

On September 1, Price's advance came within view of Fort Scott. The Missourians made off with a herd of eighty Federal mules and were pursued by two companies of Kansas cavalry as far as Dry Wood Creek. The next day, 1,200 mounted Kansans of Lane's brigade appeared on the prairie opposite the State Guardsmen, who sheltered in the timber along Dry Wood Creek. Both sides were covered by timber or tall prairie grass and remained respectfully far enough from each other to ensure that rifle fire and cannon shots did little damage—there were only a handful of casualties after two hours of lively fire. The Kansans broke off the action in the late afternoon and withdrew toward Fort Scott. State Guardsmen, according to Southern accounts, unleashed a counterattack and pursued the withdrawing (or running) enemy about a mile before turning back to camp as the sun set. The Missourians crowed that they had driven the hated Kansas Jayhawkers from the field and gained another victory for Southern arms. Lane, unnerved by reports that Price's large army was advancing on Fort Scott, immediately ordered that position evacuated. His brigade moved north to make a stand along the banks of the Little Osage River at Fort Lincoln.

The action at Dry Wood Creek hardly rose to the level of a battle. Lane had not been in danger—Old Pap was in no mood to get bogged down taking Fort Scott, either deserted or occupied. Although laying waste to Kansas was a tempting prospect, it would have to wait. Price was eager to move into the Missouri heartland before General Frémont mounted the inevitable Union counteroffensive. He kept his army on Missouri soil, turning the column northeast toward the Missouri River. Thousands of new recruits joined his swelling army as he marched into friendly territory. By then, Price had determined on an objective, Lexington.

A prosperous Missouri River town of around four thousand people, Lexington was the center of a rich Southern settlement region. Price would be viewed as a redeemer and hero there and could tap into a rich source of supplies and a huge pool of potential new recruits for his army of liberation. Lexington's strategic location on

This detail from an 1869 bird's-eye map of Lexington shows the entrenchments surrounding the Masonic College.
Library of Congress

the Missouri River made it the ideal place to receive thousands of men who had been stranded north of the Missouri River by the Union blockade of the river, and Brig. Gen. Thomas Harris and Col. Martin Green's Guardsmen were already marching to link up with Price. Best of all, according to informants who streamed daily into Price's camp with precise information on the disposition of Union forces, Lexington and its vicinity were only lightly defended by isolated detachments.

During Lyon's campaign, Union presence at Lexington consisted of five companies of German-American Home Guards commanded by a flamboyant former stage driver, Capt. F. W. Becker. In early July, Becker and his men had been briefly reinforced by a regiment of St. Louis Germans who occupied the Masonic College grounds, vacated by the secessionist forces without a fight after the defeat at Boonville. The main structure of the defunct school was a handsome colonnaded brick building on a hilltop overlooking the river. Along with a dormitory nearby, the building served as headquarters, armory, and commissary department. Soldiers began digging a ring of entrenchments around the college.

In late August, Col. Henry Routt, a Ray County lawyer who had spearheaded the seizure of Liberty Arsenal, led some 1,200 State Guard recruits to occupy the fairgrounds at Lexington. Routt also took some prominent Unionists hostage to bargain for Southern sympathizers captured earlier by the Germans. The Home Guards forted up at the Masonic College and, after much posturing but no fighting, scattered Routt's Guardsmen with three homemade mortar shells lobbed into the secessionist camp. Routt's men soon left Lexington to join Price's rapidly approaching troops.

About the same time, Union reinforcements began arriving at Lexington. The First Illinois Cavalry, under Col. Thomas Marshall, rode into town and joined the five Home Guard companies at the Masonic College, followed on August 31 by Col. James E. Mulligan and the Twenty-third Illinois Infantry from Jefferson City. These Illinois troops, raised primarily in Chicago's Irish neighborhoods, were appropriately known as the Irish Brigade. Mulligan assembled his brigade at Lexington on September 9, just three days ahead of Price and his ever-growing army. Mulligan commanded about 3,500 soldiers but had arms for only 2,700 men. Along with the Irish and local German soldiers, he had the Thirteenth Missouri Infantry under Col. Everett Peabody, Maj. R. T. Van Horn's battalion of Missouri cavalry, and Lt. Col. Benjamin Grover's Twenty-seventh Mounted Infantry. It was a diverse collection of ethnic and state soldiers from Illinois, Kansas, Iowa, and Missouri that assembled to face Price's Missourians.

When Mulligan left Jefferson City, he received orders to hold Lexington "at all hazards" until reinforcements could be sent. Confident that his command would soon increase to perhaps 10,000 troops, Colonel Mulligan immediately set his men to constructing an elaborate system of earthwork fortifications around the college that would be large enough to contain this force. Soldiers dug day and night to build a complex maze of trenches laid out with artillery lunettes (quarter moon-shaped positions for the guns) and double lines of trenches in vital sections. The perimeter of the fortifications, lined with sharpened stakes, encompassed fifteen acres.

Price neared Lexington by September 11 when the Federals briefly contested his advance at the covered bridge over Garrison Fork of Tabo Creek. Price waited until

Col. James A. Mulligan marched into Lexington with his Irish Brigade on September 9 and assumed command of the forces defending Lexington. Mulligan, a Chicago politician without military experience, courageously refused Price's demand for surrender, even though he was greatly outnumbered. *Harper's Weekly*

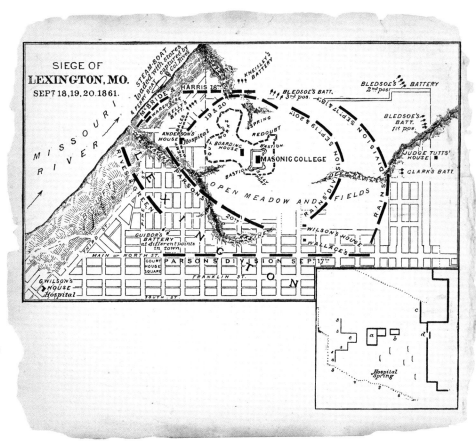

Map of the Siege of Lexington shows the Union fortifications erected around the Masonic College and the outer works of trenches dug by the Federal defenders. Price's divisions surrounded these works on all sides and over the three days of the siege tightened this cordon. Outnumbered, out of water, and with no reinforcements in sight, the Union garrison had no choice but to surrender. *"Battles and Leaders of the Civil War," Vol. 1*

the next day to drive the defenders back, then advanced to the outskirts of the town where a sharp skirmish with Federal troops took place at Machpelah Cemetery. Once more the outnumbered Yankees pulled back and retreated behind their fortifications at the college, giving up the town of Lexington to the State Guard. Two artillery batteries set up within view of the college and from mid-afternoon until dusk exchanged artillery fire with the Federals hunkered down behind their fortifications. Price's army camped outside of the town at the fairgrounds, waiting for the slow-moving infantry and the supply train to arrive. Their arrival was still days away, but with his quarry already penned up in the Masonic College fortifications, Price did not need to launch a piecemeal assault. He would wait until he had his full force, telling his subordinates at a council of war, "We've got 'em dead sure. All we have to do is watch 'em."

The "watch" extended for six days. The period was a holiday of sorts for Price's soldiers, despite nearly continuous skirmishing between parties of Federals and Guardsmen. The army was still flushed with victory, the harvest was in, and the Missouri Southerners enjoyed the warm support of the local populace. Several thousand men had flocked to the Missouri standard, and Harris and Green presented Price with more troops from northern Missouri. It was as motley an army as ever; uniforms and military weapons were almost entirely lacking. The Guardsmen dressed in homespun, or sometimes even buckskin, with ranks indicated by pieces of colored ribbon pinned on shirts. Weapons consisted of country rifles, shotguns, and old muskets, including a few flintlocks dating to the War of 1812. But word had spread rapidly through the countryside that Price had the Yankees in a trap. Once in Lexington, Price's regular forces were augmented by large numbers of pro-Southern men from the neighborhood who showed up for the exciting prospect of

a fight. Ambling into town with lunch pails and hunting rifles, they took potshots at the Federals behind their ramparts all day, breaking for lunch as they would in their own fields. By the start of the battle, it looked like an important election day in Lexington—with an accompanying turkey shoot. Perhaps 18,000 men had gathered to shoot, watch, and vent considerable frustration on the hated foe.

It was a nerve-wracking time for the trapped Federals. They scanned the horizon, watching for promised reinforcements that never appeared, worked frantically on their fortifications, and removed cornfields, trees, and anything that obstructed their fields of fire, including several houses near the college that might conceal snipers, which were torched. As the days wore on, the food supplies dwindled. Worse still was the diminishing water supply inside the fortification, supplied by cisterns around the college. Not only were there several thousand thirsty men within the compound but also a nearly equal number of thirsty horses and mules. It was still possible for Federal parties to replenish supplies at the Missouri River or two nearby springs, but Price's men closed off access to these sources by September 17. Mulligan had not thought it necessary to dig wells, a decision that shortly caused much misery and suffering for his soldiers.

Price knew that with every passing day, the arrival of a Federal relief force became more likely. By Wednesday, September 18, he was ready to intensify the siege. He now had 10,000 to 12,000 men arrayed in seven divisions and outnumbered the enemy at least four to one. Price formed his ragtag troops at the fairgrounds that morning and marched them to the sounds of beating drums and cheering

This painting by an obscure Hungarian artist named Domenico is a rare example of a work of art executed while the Battle of Lexington was in progress. Domenico set his easel up on the northeast side of the battlefield and captured the moment when Gen. Sterling Price's entire force was in action, firing heated cannonballs into the Masonic College and adjacent dormitory to make them burn. *Used by permission, State Historical Society of Missouri, Columbia*

through town to the Masonic College. The Lexington brass band played a recently composed tune called "Dixie." As Colonel Mulligan later recalled: "They came as one dark moving mass, their guns beaming in the sun, their banners waving, and their drums beating—everywhere, as far as we could see, were men, men, men, approaching grandly. Our men stood firm behind the breastworks, none trembled or paled, and a solemn silence prevailed." The Eighth Division, under Gen. James S. Rains, marched to the east side of the Masonic College fortification. The Third Division, commanded by Col. Congreve Jackson, marched down the main road and detoured to a position on the left of Rains. Gen. Mosby M. Parsons's Sixth Division wheeled around to the western end of town and marched up Third Street to form a line to the left of Col. Jackson along Main Street. Gen. A. E. Steen's Fifth Division established a position on the west side of the fortifications. The Fourth Division temporarily led by Col. Benjamin Rives, the Second Division under the command of Gen. Thomas Harris, and Gen. James McBride's Seventh Division took up positions along the northern edge of town and the riverfront, completing the encirclement of the dug-in Federals.

Before he opened the next phase of the battle, Price sent a demand for surrender to Mulligan. Although Mulligan was not a professional military man, he was brave, his blood was up, and he still believed reinforcements were coming to his rescue. He replied to Price, "If you want us, you must take us."

Rebuffed, Price opened the battle with the guns of Henry Guibor, Churchill Clark, James Kneisley, and Ephraim Kelly, sixteen cannons in all, positioned in a great arc around the Yankee position. The artillery rained metal on the Federals for more than nine hours.

A favorite target was the Masonic College building, which they tried to set ablaze with superheated cannonballs. This effort failed thanks to a courageous teenaged Yankee who shoveled each red-hot ball out a window. Meanwhile, from every place of concealment, riflemen squeezed off shot after shot all day long, pouring a murderous hail of bullets into the Union fortifications.

Oliver Anderson's mansion marked the western side of the battlefield. The Anderson family had been evicted by Union authorities by the time of the battle, and the house was commandeered for use as a Union hospital. It held 120 wounded and sick, and a yellow flag flying atop the roof signified its neutral status. The Anderson house nevertheless was attacked by Colonel Rives's Guardsmen, who had moved up from the waterfront in building-to-building fighting, driving the Federals before them toward the hospital. The

Oliver Anderson, prominent businessman and slaveholder, built his mansion in 1853. A well-known Southern sympathizer, Anderson and his family were evicted from the house when Unionists occupied Lexington. At the time of the battle, the house was being used as a hospital and sustained damage that can still be seen. The house is part of the Battle of Lexington State Historic Site and is open for tours. *James M. Denny, Missouri Department of Natural Resources*

Southerners later said that they had received rifle fire from the house, making it a legitimate target. The Anderson house also had great tactical value as high ground from which State Guard sharpshooters could deliver withering fire into the Union entrenchments. Whatever the case, Rives's men advanced from the west side and overran the building with little difficulty, scattering its defenders by noontime.

Mulligan, incensed by the capture of the hospital and considering it a breach of the etiquette of war, asked for volunteers to retake the building. Two Missouri companies flatly refused. A suicidal dash across one hundred yards of open ground through a hail of enemy fire held little appeal, and with thousands of State Guard in that sector of the battlefield, there seemed little chance the Anderson house could be held once taken. One of Mulligan's Irish companies, the Montgomery Guards, finally stepped forward. Susan McCausland, a Lexington resident, witnessed the courageous charge of those 80 men: "I had been [observing] but a very short time when a double line of human forms appeared on top of the embankment and rushed over, followed by the serried ranks of others, all firing upon the house as they hurtled down upon it. And how they fell! Some of them, on the way, and [they] lay there amongst the flowers of the garden until all was over and the bodies could be moved. And how they yelled as they charged!" Twenty-five or more of the assault party fell as they raced across the killing zone, but the survivors, in a murderous rage, burst into the Anderson house and drove out the defenders. The scars left by gunfire exchanged in the stairwell may be seen to this day. Four Guardsmen attempted to surrender; but the enraged Federals executed three of them at the foot of the stairs. Late in the afternoon, the State Guard retook the house in fierce room-to-room fighting. As darkness fell over the battlefield, the night sky was pierced by the flash of cannon fire. Buildings hit by Federal hot shot burned and smoldered, casting a lurid red glow over the town.

The Irish Brigade's charge on the Anderson house occurred on the first day of the battle after the residence, in use as a Federal hospital, was overrun by State Guardsmen. Considering this a breach of military etiquette, Mulligan asked for volunteers to retake the house. The Montgomery Guards of the Irish Brigade accomplished this in a bloody charge.
Harper's Weekly

On the third day of the Battle of Lexington, someone, perhaps Gen. Sterling Price himself, had the inspired idea to use hemp bales as a moving breastworks to make an assault on the Federal ramparts without the heavy casualties that usually resulted from charges against fortified positions. *John R. Musick, "Stories from Missouri," American Book Company, 1897*

The next day, Thursday, September 19, dawned on a desperate situation for the Yankee defenders at the Masonic College. The soldiers were nearly out of food, and their water supply was getting critically low in the late summer heat. Three thousand animals kept within the fortifications had nearly drained the limited water supply of the garrison's cisterns. The Southern cordon tightening around the garrison prevented nightly forays out of the fortifications to water sources. The only relief for the thirsty troops came by way of a morning thunderstorm. The soldiers captured the rain in their blankets and wrung the precious drops into cups. Increasing the misery within the fortifications was the overpowering odor of horses killed by artillery shells and rifle fire. Their putrefying carcasses created an unbearable stench, but it was the lack of reinforcements that caused morale to suffer the most.

Frémont had indeed sent a flurry of marching orders to many units, but only one detachment actually made a real attempt to aid Mulligan. Brig. Gen. Samuel Sturgis marched at the head of 1,100 men toward Lexington from the north and sent a courier to inform Mulligan that he was on the way. However, the message fell into Price's hands when the courier was captured, and Price sent General Parsons and 3,000 men across the river to ambush the relief column. Sturgis, in turn, learned of the trap being set and turned away without a fight. There would be no help from Frémont or anyone else now; Mulligan and his besieged soldiers were on their own.

Southern riflemen close to the fortifications led the action on the second day, sniping the trenches and pouring a continuous volley of rifle fire into the enemy position. Any Federal moving about or poking his head too far above the ramparts ran the risk of being picked off, but somehow they managed to return fire amidst the deluge of Southern bullets. Meanwhile, the incessant artillery bombardment continued. One stray cannonball overshot its mark and struck a column of the courthouse where the damage it caused can still be seen. By the end of the day, Price's men had drawn the noose around the Masonic College still tighter.

In warehouses on the Missouri River wharf below the Anderson house, Price's men discovered a number of hemp bales and muscled some of them uphill for use as breastworks. There were many claimants, Price among them, for the brilliant idea to use the large bales as a rolling fortification. No matter whose concept it was, the idea proved to be the tactical inspiration that would bring the Battle of Lexington to its unusual and celebrated conclusion. One story has it that Price, urged by his zealous subordinates in a war council to unleash an all-out storming of the ramparts, replied: "There is no use in killing the boys now. Poor fellows! They may, some of them at least, be killed soon enough." Price realized that these bales of hemp could be used as a moving shield from which to launch a final assault on the Federal works with relatively little loss of his troops' lives. Late in the day on September 19, men from the commands of Thomas Harris and Benjamin Rives began hauling dozens of the heavy bales toward the Anderson house, where they were arranged in double rows, like large wings on either side of the building.

The batteries of Bledsoe and Clark opened the final day of battle on Friday morning, September 20, with a barrage of shot and shell directed at the Masonic College building. The besieged Federals, however, took more notice of a movement they saw taking place on the west side of the battlefield. There they saw a long snake-like line of hemp bales moving slowly and inexorably toward them as Price's men, concealed behind them, pushed and rolled the ponderous bales forward. Rifle fire had no effect at all on the dense bales. Even cannonballs did no more than rock them slightly. The Yankees tried firing red-hot cannonballs hoping to set them on fire, but Price's men, anticipating this, had soaked the hemp with water.

By 9 a.m., one end of the hemp bale line had been maneuvered close to a lunette in the northwest corner of the Union fortification. A group of Southerners under Col. Martin Green left the cover of the bales and boldly charged the outer line of breastworks. Major Becker's Home Guard companies, along with a company of the Irish Brigade, managed to drive the Southerners back. For the next four hours, the hemp bale breastworks slowly rolled toward Mulligan's lines. The Federals continued to fire cannon shot into the hemp bales, but the line moved inexorably forward. Every Southern rifle unleashed its deadly fire. Around 1 p.m. there was another assault on Becker's line. This time the Home Guard sallied from their own lines to meet the attackers. After a few minutes of intense hand-to-hand fighting, the Southerners were stopped, and the battered defenders withdrew again to their entrenchments. Shortly afterward, a white flag appeared in this sector of the Union fortifications, and firing gradually ceased. While the purpose of this flag was evidently to arrange a temporary truce to retrieve the dead and wounded from the last action, Price's forces mistook it for a flag of surrender. The German troops, however, had seen how hopelessly outnumbered they were. They fled in a panic to the innermost works at the college and refused to continue the fight. A second white flag was raised, this time by Major Becker, the only officer of his rank left unwounded.

A line of hemp bales, soaked in water to prevent red-hot cannonballs from setting them on fire, slowly snaked toward the Federal forces' positions. Besieged Federal forces opened fire but were ineffectual on the advancing line; even cannon shot only caused the bales to rock a little. *"Battles and Leaders of the Civil War," Vol. 1*

Although angered by Becker's unauthorized actions, Mulligan realized that the hour of capitulation had come. By this time, the embattled garrison had been under fire for fifty-two continuous hours. Without water or rations, a nearly exhausted supply of ammunition, and most of the officers, including Mulligan himself, wounded, the Union officer had little choice but surrender or annihilation. Reluctantly and with tears welling in his eyes, the hard-fighting Mulligan sent word to Price that he was prepared to accede to Price's terms for surrender. Then the Federals marched out of their trenches, stacked arms, and were lined up to hear addresses by General Price and Governor-in-exile Claiborne Jackson.

The governor had spent the previous two months in Richmond conferring with Jefferson Davis, in Memphis meeting with Maj. Gen. Leonidas Polk, and at New Madrid, which was now occupied by Confederate forces. After the victory at Wilson's Creek, he had determined to link up with Price. He finally caught up with the Missouri army just before the battle opened at Lexington. Jackson excoriated Mulligan's defeated forces, berated their presence in Missouri, and chided them for meddling in Missouri affairs. He warned them to go home and tend to their own business. Price was a more gracious victor, telling the enemy, "You were the hardest troops to capture I have ever seen."

After the surrender, most of the prisoners were escorted across the river and paroled on the condition that they not take up arms against Missouri or the Confederacy. Mulligan refused parole and was held by the Southerners to exchange for a Rebel prisoner of war of similar rank. The stout-hearted Irishman was subsequently exchanged for Brig. Gen. Daniel Marsh Frost, captured by Lyon at Camp Jackson back in May.

The casualty count at Lexington was 25 killed and 75 wounded on Price's side, while the federals lost 39 killed and 120 wounded, and Mulligan's entire force captured. The immediate gain from the battle amounted to five artillery pieces, 3,000 rifles, and 750 horses, all of which were highly beneficial to the under-equipped Missouri army.

A substantial amount of money was recovered, as well. On September 7, at the order of Col. T. A. Marshall, $960,159.60 had been seized from the Farmers' Bank of Missouri at Lexington—$165,659.60 in gold coin and the rest in notes. The

boxes and cases of money were transported to the Union fortifications and buried under Mulligan's tent. The Unionists had seized the money for the express purpose of keeping it from falling into the hands of Jackson and Price, where it could be used to serve the rebellion. Following the surrender, however, the funds were recovered and delivered to Price. Although the State Guard was short of funds to buy weapons and supplies and to pay volunteers, neither Price nor Jackson seemed inclined to "borrow" this vast sum and put it to the service of the Southern cause. The funds were returned to the Farmers' Bank. They did reserve $37,377.20, an amount authorized by the state legislature back in March.

Lexington was Price's greatest victory. He became a hero throughout the entire South and came to personify the struggle in Missouri. Newspapers hailed his triumph at Lexington as the greatest Southern victory in the war, second only to Manassas (Bull Run), Virginia. Price was at the top of his form and at the height of his personal glory.

However, the first year of the war was not yet over. Lexington turned out to be the high tide of the Southern cause in Missouri, but it did not become the springboard for an offensive to regain control of Missouri's heartland and restore its political establishment. Victory along the Missouri River produced no long-term gains. Indeed, without support from the Confederate armies, Price could not linger long on the Missouri River, let alone begin operations in the lower valley aimed at Jefferson City and St. Louis.

Had Hardee and Pillow united forces and advanced on St. Louis, Frémont might have been too busy defending his headquarters to deal with Price. Had McCulloch and Price cooperated, they might have established a formidable base in western Missouri from which to launch assaults toward the state capital and St.

Governor-in-exile Claiborne Jackson addressed the captured Federal soldiers, who had held out bravely for three days without water or reinforcement. Jackson berated them for meddling in Missouri affairs. More gracious, General Price told them, "You were the hardest troops to capture I have ever seen." *Harper's Weekly*

THE CIVIL WAR'S FIRST BLOOD

Louis while Hardee and Pillow attacked from the south. Missouri's top secessionist officials—Governor Jackson, Lt. Gov. Thomas Reynolds, and General Price—ardently advocated this strategy, but their pleas fell on deaf ears everywhere in the Confederate high command. The Confederacy had already conceded control of Missouri to the North.

As it turned out, Price stayed at Lexington for only ten days following his victory. General Frémont assembled a massive army of 38,000 troops and was already moving toward Lexington. In the face of this threat, Price had little choice but to withdraw again into the southwest quarter of Missouri. Before departing, Governor Jackson issued a call for members of the deposed General Assembly to convene in Neosho on October 21 to draw up an ordinance of secession and formally carry Missouri into the Confederacy. At the same time, he dispatched emissaries to Richmond to negotiate an offensive-defensive treaty between the Confederate government and the sovereign state of Missouri. At Lexington, thousands of new recruits had rallied to the standard, but there was no way to arm or feed them. Price reluctantly sent home thousands of these sunshine patriots who had showed up for the battle to await his future call. Although better equipped, courtesy of the enemy, than at the beginning of its campaign, Price's army ultimately returned to southwestern Missouri about the same size as it had been a month earlier.

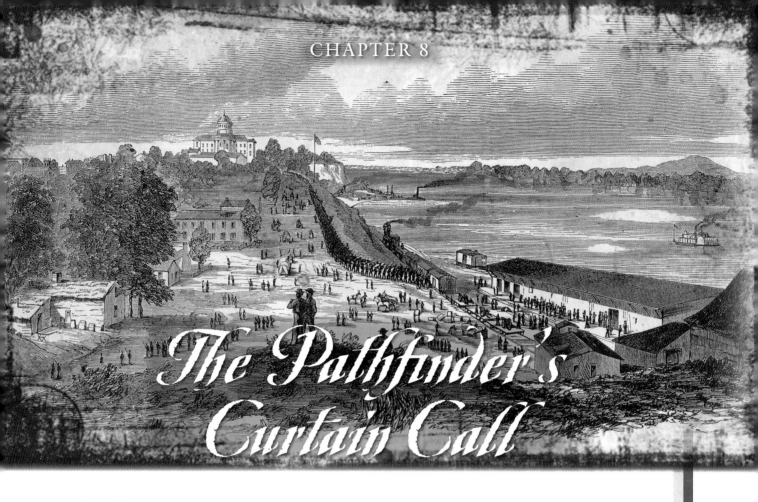

CHAPTER 8

The Pathfinder's Curtain Call

MAJ. GEN. JOHN C. FRÉMONT'S position as Union commander of the Department of the West was already in jeopardy before the disaster at Lexington. Since assuming command, he had faced huge problems with limited resources, and he seemed to have had too little luck and not enough tact to get a grip on the job. Every course of action he followed seemed to be wrong. When he reached St. Louis, the enemy seemed poised to attack on two fronts. Brig. Gen. Nathaniel Lyon was in southwest Missouri facing a numerically superior Southern army, while Brig. Gen. Benjamin Prentiss found himself in a similar situation in the southeast corner of the state. Both generals pled urgently for more soldiers, but Frémont did not have enough troops.

He chose to reinforce Prentiss, reasoning that a threat to federal control of the Mississippi River and St. Louis seemed the more important priority. He suggested that Lyon withdraw to Rolla. But Lyon chose instead to give battle to an enemy more than twice the size of his forces and lost both the battle and his life. When the Confederate invasion of southeast Missouri failed to materialize, it looked as if Frémont had elected to deal with an imaginary threat and failed to deal with the real one. To his critics, especially Frank Blair, it appeared that he had deserted Lyon in his hour of need and handed southwest Missouri to the secessionists.

The Lexington disaster seemed further proof that Frémont had lost control of the situation in Missouri. He seemed to be undoing the achievements of Blair and Lyon in securing Union control of the state. Hamilton Gamble wrote angrily to a correspondent that Frémont "is incomprehensible to me. We have lost Lexington. We will soon lose the whole state." In fairness, Frémont had been well aware of the importance of holding Lexington and had sent orders to his subordinates to hasten to relieve Colonel Mulligan's

Frémont began assembling his Army of the West below the state capitol in October 1861. *Frank Leslie's Illustrated Newspaper*

Famous as the Pathfinder of the Rocky Mountain West and married to Sen. Thomas Hart Benton's daughter, Jesse, John C. Frémont seemed to be the perfect choice to command in Missouri. *John McElroy, "The Struggle for Missouri"*

besieged garrison. Unfortunately for Frémont, these subordinates failed to grasp the urgency of the situation and left Mulligan to his fate. Col. Jefferson C. Davis commanded nearly 10,000 men at Jefferson City and could have moved them to Lexington by rail or Missouri River steamboats or by marching through the rich agricultural country. But he lingered in Jefferson City, claiming a lack of wagons to form his supply train.

In northeast Missouri where there was no significant enemy force left to fight, Gen. John Pope might have dogged Martin Green all the way to Lexington with the major portion of his command, but Pope remained on guard along the Hannibal and St. Joseph Railroad, though he did dispatch the Third Iowa and Sixteenth Illinois toward Lexington. However, when these units encountered a large enemy force at Blue Mills Landing, near Kansas City, they fell back. Gen. Samuel Sturgis, marching from Mexico, was the only Federal commander to come within sight of Lexington but had no way to get his 1,100 men across the Missouri River. He retreated when he learned that Price was preparing to ambush him.

No one was more aware than John Charles Frémont that his job hung by a thread. He could no longer hope that subordinates might repair the damage caused by the defeat at Lexington. Of the three major military disasters that had thus far befallen the Union war effort—First Bull Run, Wilson's Creek, and now Lexington—two of them had taken place in his department. He boldly announced that he would take personal command of the force that would move against Price. Commanding Gen. Winfield Scott conveyed Lincoln's expectations: "Your dispatch of this day is received. The President is glad you are hastening to the scene of action. His words are, 'He expects you to repair the disaster at Lexington without loss of time.'"

Frémont's problems were compounded by the fact that he not only confronted a formidable enemy in his front in Sterling Price and his army but now also had an array of enemies at home in his rear. Frank Blair had lost faith in Frémont's ability to control the military situation in Missouri and believed the commanding general was unable to grasp the fundamentals of what needed to be done. "Oh for one hour of our dead Lyon," he lamented, his anguish intensified by the fact that he and his family had urged Lincoln to appoint the Pathfinder to command the Department of the West in the first place.

Lincoln was hearing complaints from many quarters about Frémont's failures to devise a coherent plan of action to defeat the enemy in his department. Those disaffected with Frémont included Edward Bates and Montgomery Blair, the two Missourians in his cabinet. Hamilton Gamble, the provisional governor of Missouri, also expressed his misgivings about Frémont to the president.

In early September, Lincoln sent Montgomery Blair, Frank's brother, and Quartermaster Gen. Montgomery Meigs to St. Louis to investigate allegations of mismanagement and graft in Frémont's department. Lincoln personally requested Maj. Gen. David Hunter to join Frémont's department and lend the benefit of his counsel and experience, because "he is losing the confidence of men near him, whose support any man in his position must have to be successful. His cardinal mistake is that he isolates himself, and allows nobody to see him; and by which he does not know what is going on in the very matter he is dealing with. He needs to have by his side a man of large experience."

Frémont knew that Frank Blair was disseminating a dim view of the commanding officer's policies to officials in Washington. He arrested Blair and jailed him at the St. Louis arsenal—not once but twice. Montgomery Blair suspected that this rash

Montgomery Blair was a member of the Blair family that had been influential in national politics since the times of Andrew Jackson. Montgomery was presently serving as Lincoln's postmaster general and working closely with his brother, Frank, to keep Missouri in the Union column. The Blair family had helped make the rise of John C. Frémont possible and would shortly help to orchestrate his downfall. *Used by permission, State Historical Society of Missouri, Columbia*

Frémont doted on European-trained officers. He and Sigel, on left, were extremely popular among German Americans in Missouri, despite the demonstrated incompetence of both. *Carte de Visite of an engraving by John W. Scholten of St. Louis, John Bradbury Collection*

and impolitic action was
done at the urging of the Pathfinder's meddling
and vindictive wife, Jesse Benton Frémont—"Gen'l Jesse," as Blair termed her.

Despite the rising crescendo of calls for Frémont's removal, Lincoln still hesitated, perhaps reluctant to alienate the radical faction that remained intensely loyal to Frémont. Much to the chagrin of Edward Bates and Montgomery Blair, the president gave his commander in the West one more opportunity to redeem or ruin himself in the seething, chaotic, and threatened department.

Frémont intended to make the most of his final chance and set to work laying plans to advance on Price with an overwhelming force. Gen. David Hunter, designated to command the First Division, took up a position at Versailles with 9,750 men. The Second Division, commanded by Gen. John Pope, was dispatched to Boonville with 9,220 men. The Third Division, comprised of 7,980 soldiers under Gen. Franz Sigel, was posted at Sedalia. Gen. Alexander Asboth, a Hungarian veteran of the Revolution of 1848 and another of the foreign officers appointed by Frémont, led 6,451 troops in the Fourth Division at Tipton, which constituted the reserve. Gen. Justus McKinstry commanded 5,388 troops in the Fifth Division, the center of the huge army, five miles west of Tipton at Syracuse. In total, the divisions added up to 38,789 men, a veritable *Grande Armée* and the largest Union army

Maj. Gen. David S. Hunter, a veteran Regular Army officer, was appointed by Lincoln to share his long experience with General Frémont, but the commanding general never consulted him. *Library of Congress*

Frémont set up headquarters at Tipton while he assembled a supply train big enough to take care of his massive army. It was mid-October before the army was ready to depart Tipton. By that time, Price was leisurely withdrawing from Lexington. *Frank Leslie's Illustrated Newspaper*

ever assembled in Missouri. In addition, Gen. James Lane had 2,500 troops on the western border who could harry Price's flank, and Gen. Samuel Sturgis was in Kansas City with another 3,000 men.

All that remained was for this overwhelming force to close with Price, bring him to battle, and annihilate his Guardsmen. But this proved the rub. Frémont, one of only four major generals in the Union army, had little military experience. Previous to receiving his departmental command, he had never led more than a few hundred men. It was the same for most of his field officers, with the exception of some of the foreign veterans of the Revolution of 1848. Many of the Regular Army officers had been mere lieutenants or captains at the war's outset. Now they commanded as colonels or generals but without the leadership experience to train and maneuver large bodies of soldiers.

An army such as Frémont's, had it moved with swiftness and decisiveness, might have gained a position in Price's front and blocked his retreat while the remainder of the army fell on his rear. But northern military leaders with real ability, such as Ulysses S. Grant and William T. Sherman, had not yet emerged. (Grant was just beginning to make his mark on the eastern side of the state while Frémont was chasing Price.)

Movements of armies were still done by the book. No one marched out without first forming a supply train. The idea of living off the bounty of the land, as Grant later did with such brilliance in the Vicksburg campaign, was as yet inconceivable. It took Frémont until mid-October to put together the huge supply train that accompanied his mammoth army. By then, he had established his headquarters in the field at Tipton.

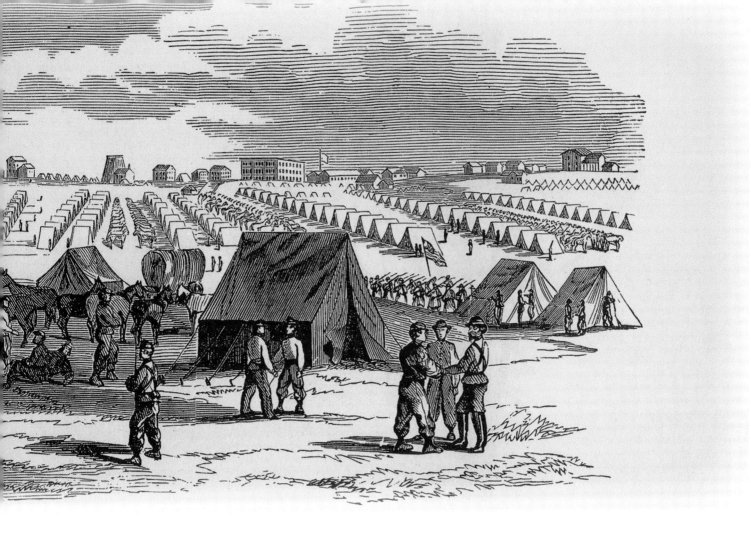

Sterling Price had long since departed Lexington by the time Frémont was at last ready to set his army in motion. Thanks to Federal inaction, Price spent ten leisurely days following the victory at Lexington gathering supplies in the richest part of Missouri. He knew that he had to retreat. Although his army had swelled to more than double its original size by the time of the battle, he had to send 13,000 would-be recruits back home for want of any way to quarter or feed them over the coming winter.

Price left Lexington with 7,000 men, a gain of perhaps a thousand over the number of Guardsmen who had marched northward from Springfield a little more than a month earlier. The army moved at a leisurely pace of fifteen miles a day, reaching Osceola on the Osage River after a march of nine days.

The formerly prosperous town of Osceola was now a smoldering ruin. On September 23, the town had received a visit from the "Grim Chieftain," Jim Lane. The Kansan had discreetly waited for Price and his army to move on to Lexington before making a foray into Missouri with 1,500 Kansas soldiers. Lane planned to wreak a little havoc on Price's probable route of withdrawal back to southwest Missouri, chastising disloyal Missourians and liberating their slaves. He and his cohorts were also equally bent on liberating the contents of banks, stores, houses, and barnyards along his route. What could not be carried off would be burned.

Along the way to Osceola, Lane and his men pillaged Butler, Harrisonville, and Clinton. But the real prize was Osceola, the head of navigation on the Osage River, the county seat of St. Clair County, and a flourishing place before Lane showed up. Steamboats deposited a wealth of products at the riverfront, and at times, as many as a hundred wagons filled with all kinds of goods would be lined up along

Sen. Jim Lane had been hated by Missourians since Bloody Kansas days. Lane returned the favor. His Kansas soldiers chastised western Missourians by liberating their slaves and as much of their personal property as could be hauled back to Kansas and by burning Osceola and other communities to the ground. *Library of Congress*

the streets. The town could boast of five blacksmith shops, twelve to fifteen retail stores, hotels, a newspaper, a tanyard, and, of course, a bank. The handsome brick courthouse had cost fifteen thousand dollars to build.

Lane, who had brought two cannons with him, had little trouble scattering the company of State Guardsmen in the area. He and his men entered Osceola and began to systematically plunder the defenseless town. The bank safe was blown open and its contents emptied; then the Jayhawkers proceeded to the contents of stores and houses. The troops piled wagons full of merchandise and furniture. Many of the Kansans got drunk on whiskey discovered among the spoils, and they were also heaped on the wagons. Lane reportedly reserved a fine piano and a quantity of silk dresses for himself. The rest was burned, ostensibly to keep the supplies from falling into Price's hands. For good measure, Lane ordered the entire town to be put to the torch. The courthouse and all its records went up in flames. Ironically, one of the few houses that escaped destruction was that of Lane's U.S. Senate colleague, Waldo P. Johnson, shortly to be expelled from that body due to his Southern sympathies. Johnson then joined the Confederate army, received a wound at the Battle of Pea Ridge, and ultimately served as Missouri's representative in the Confederate Senate.

A third of the Osceola merchants who saw their property burnt and livelihoods destroyed were loyal Union men—a fact that mattered not at all to Lane and his Jayhawkers, who destroyed loyal and disloyal establishments alike in the town's business district. The lack of distinction between the loyal and disloyal among citizens, a policy first set in motion by John Pope in northern Missouri, was taken to a new level by Lane. His policy, which became the watchword of Jayhawkerism, was that "everything disloyal from a Shanghai rooster to a Durham cow must be cleaned out."

But no Jayhawker had to worry much about the "disloyal" part. All Missourians were treated alike, and all property was considered ripe for looting. Lines of wagons loaded with booty stolen from Missouri citizens, no matter their political persuasions, soon rolled toward such hated strongholds of abolitionism as Lawrence, Kansas, Lane's lair. Perhaps some old scores from the Bleeding Kansas days were settled on the day Lane destroyed Osceola, but Missourians would not forget what the Jayhawkers had done. The time for settling their scores was not long in coming. As the Civil War gradually revealed its full extent, the Kansas-Missouri border would become a unique and hellish place with its own special brand of intense hatred.

During the march of the Kansas brigade, scores of slaves seeking escape from their masters swarmed to Lane. The Grim Chieftain was well ahead of the rest of the North in seeing the war not only as means to preserve the Union but also as means to free the slaves of the rebellious South. In Missouri's case, that meant the rebellious Southern population. The previous July he had proclaimed in the Senate that slavery could not survive the march of the Union armies. On October 3, he wrote to Gen. Samuel Sturgis, "Confiscation of slaves and other property, which can be made useful to the Army, should follow treason as the thunder peal follows the lightning flash." It didn't matter to Lane and his fellow Jayhawkers that the governments of Missouri and Kansas were supposed to be on the same side or that many Missouri slaveholders were Unionists. Gamble's government, with Lincoln's blessing, had assured these powerful and wealthy citizens that their loyalty would be rewarded by using the force of the government and army to protect their slave property. But when Lane's wagonloads of plunder made their way back to Kansas, scores of slaves accompanied the train, often driving their former masters' teams and wagons. They

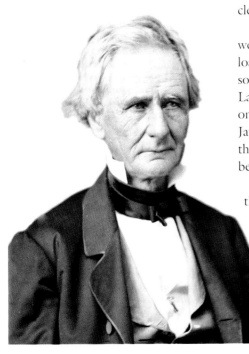

Simon Cameron, the Secretary of War, paid a visit to General Frémont's Tipton encampment. The secretary bore an order relieving Frémont from command but relented when the general pled for a chance to redeem himself in battle.
Library of Congress

soon made themselves useful as teamsters or cooks.

While the ashes of Osceola yet smoldered, Price's army took three days to ford the Osage. There was no hurry, for Frémont had yet to begin his pursuit. While the Pathfinder was still at Tipton, he received a visit from the secretary of war, Simon Cameron, and the adjutant general, Lorenzo Thomas. It was hardly a friendly social call. Lincoln was alarmed by the stream of reports pouring into Washington concerning financial and other irregularities within Frémont's department, not to mention the department commander's seeming inability to exert military control. He sent Cameron and Thomas to investigate the state of affairs in the Department of the West. Cameron carried with him a signed presidential order relieving Frémont of his command, but Lincoln left it to Cameron to decide whether or not to execute it.

Cameron and Thomas stopped in St. Louis to visit with Blair and allies of Governor Gamble. What they heard from these sources about the conduct of affairs in the department hardly encouraged them regarding Frémont's capabilities. Lincoln had sent along a letter to Gen. Samuel Curtis asking him to be forthcoming with Cameron and Thomas in his assessment of the Pathfinder's management of the department. Curtis's analysis was succinct and devastating: The commander "lacks the intelligence, the experience and the sagacity necessary to his command." Curtis reported that it was easier to share his advice and opinions with Commander in Chief Winfield Scott in Washington than to confer with Frémont in St. Louis. Frémont would not consult on military matters or divulge his plans to him.

In Tipton, Cameron and Thomas sought Gen. David Hunter's appraisal. Lincoln had sent the general to Frémont so that the commanding general would have the benefit of Hunter's extensive experience and counsel, but Hunter passed on much the same story that they heard from Curtis—confusion reigned within the command, and Frémont was utterly incompetent. True to pattern, Frémont never consulted Hunter or sought his opinion. John Pope, who had done little to help Frémont, drove his own nails into his commander's coffin by declaring to Hunter that if his soldiers moved forward against Price under the present confused conditions and lack of supplies, only "one half of these troops will ever return alive."

One of Curtis's most trenchant criticisms of Frémont was that "he was no more bound by law than by the winds." Indeed, the initial investigations of irregularities within the department revealed a cavalier disregard of rules and regulations. Although Frémont had no authority to appoint officers, no less than forty-two officers—including a colonel, three majors, eight captains, and several lieutenants—received commissions and pay by his personal order.

Particularly disturbing were the financial irregularities in the quartermaster's department, which had accumulated a whopping debt of $4,506,309.73 on Frémont's watch. Firms with connections to the Pathfinder's California cronies sold forage at inflated prices, then transported it from St. Louis to Jefferson City, an abundant countryside where it could have been purchased much more cheaply.

Corruption extended to the hospitals, where sick and wounded soldiers received rotten blankets, and to the cavalry service, into which the army received hundreds of horses that turned out to be blind, sick nags. Armaments were not much better—one colonel discovered that only twenty guns in a shipment of one hundred would actually fire. The weapons were part of a large order of such guns procured by Frémont in Europe in a deal by which a San Francisco business associate pocketed a handsome thirty thousand dollar profit.

The worst offender in Frémont's command appeared to be his quartermaster, sticky-fingered Justus McKinstry, who devised a scheme involving overpayments

Lorenzo Thomas, adjutant general of the United States, accompanied Secretary Cameron to Missouri. Like Cameron, Thomas was dismayed at the reports concerning Frémont's administration. *Library of Congress*

As Frémont's quartermaster, Justus McKinstry was said to have presided over "a system of reckless expenditure and fraud, perhaps unheard of before in the history of the world" before becoming the first United States officer to be cashiered during the war for fiscal misfeasance. *Rossiter Johnson, "Campfire and Battlefield," New York, Bryan, Taylor & Co. 1894*

and kickbacks that Gen. George B. McClellan described as "a system of reckless expenditure and fraud, perhaps unheard of before in the history of the world" (surely an exaggeration in the vast arena of military profiteering). Nevertheless, McKinstry had cooked up an arrangement whereby the St. Louis firm of Child, Pratt, and Fox received contracts for purchases at markups of up to 300 percent. Other manufacturers had to deal with Child, Pratt, and Fox rather than directly with the government. A share of their lucrative profits returned under the table to McKinstry, and the corporate officers expressed their gratitude to McKinstry by setting him up with a fine horse and buggy, providing a pony for his son, and giving his wife an extravagant silver service that cost three thousand dollars.

McKinstry's dealings proved too slimy even for Frémont, who removed him from his office by promoting him to brigadier general and giving him command of a division in the campaign against Price. Ultimately, the corrupt quartermaster's overpriced chickens came home to roost, and McKinstry became the first general in the Union army to be summarily booted out of the service. One unanticipated benefit came in the wake of the mess left by McKinstry. Among the officers sent to the department was an energetic young quartermaster, champing for a field command, by the name of Capt. Philip H. Sheridan, who would finish his military career as the leader of the entire United States army.

At Tipton, Thomas and Cameron found scarcely any means of transportation to move the forces assembled there. General Hunter had been told to bring forty-one wagons with him from Jefferson City, but he only had forty mules to pull them. To move forward, he needed one hundred wagons but was ordered to march without them. A cavalry regiment carried cartridges in their pockets for lack of pouches—ammunition that was soaked and ruined during a dismal, rainy march from Jefferson City. The men marched along a muddy dirt road running parallel to the Pacific Railroad that might have transported them faster and drier. The same troops went without food for twenty-four hours, only to be given spoiled beef.

Given the evident confusion that reigned, Secretary Cameron had more than enough justification to hand Lincoln's order of dismissal to Frémont. When the general realized he was now nearly out of options, he feigned being shocked by the revelation that his dismissal letter had already been drafted. He pled with Cameron that, since he had his army in the field, he ought to be allowed to come to military conclusions with Price. Cameron finally decided to allow Frémont to conduct his campaign, but he warned him that should the general fail to intercept Price, he would forfeit his command.

Catching Price was a large order. By the time Frémont's army got underway, Price's army was already one hundred miles away at Greenfield. On the eve of departure, a member of the Sixth Iowa Infantry described the condition of the army that was about to set forth, "With only wagon transportation, an inferior quality of unserviceable foreign-made guns, a lamentable lack of military method in the plans for the campaign, a want of confidence and harmony among the commanders who were to lead the army, and in many regiments, discipline little better than that of a huge mob, the orders were promulgated to commence the grand forward movement into the heart of the enemy's country."

Despite incomplete preparations, the five divisions lumbered into motion. Miry roads made the going slow, especially for the long supply trains. Foragers ranged widely throughout the countryside, impressing every wagon and team they could lay their hands on and carrying off anything suitable to feed an army. In theory, every item taken from Union men was either paid for in cash or certificates issued to the owner of the appropriated property. But widespread pilferage led to general

The ponderous march of Frémont's army
allowed Price's forces to withdraw leisurely
from Lexington to Springfield.
Harper's Weekly

orders reminding the troops that while their commanding general intended to go after the enemy with the utmost vigor, "It is equally his aim to inspire confidence in the loyal inhabitants of this State, and to assure others of protection and immunity if they return to their allegiance."

Cleaning them out of their possessions hardly furthered this goal. According to one observer, "There is scarcely a feathered biped left within five miles of either side of their marches." Anguished women would entreat the general, as he rode by, to return a husband and team that soldiers had commandeered. According to a series in *Atlantic Monthly* by William Dorsheimer, one woman, claiming to be a Union-loving "widder," protested to Frémont that she had given the soldiers all they wanted: "I gi'n 'em turkeys and chickens and eggs and butter and bread. And I never charged 'em anything for it. They tuk all my corn, and I never said nuthing." But when the soldiers pilfered her ox-chains, that was the last straw. "I can't do any work without them chains; they's 'a' better tuk my teams with 'em, too." The woman thought it would cost five dollars to replace the chains, but the bemused general rewarded her with a gold eagle. It is doubtful that very many other matriarchs of cleaned-out farmsteads were so handsomely recompensed.

Gen. Franz Sigel, who led the advance of the army to Warsaw, had been energetic in forming his makeshift train. In it were mule teams and ox teams and even horses, mules, and oxen hitched together. In addition to army wagons, Dorsheimer noted, there were box wagons, lumber wagons, hay racks, buggies, carriages—"in fact, every kind of animal and every description of vehicle which could be found in the country."

The Osage River formed the biggest obstacle to the forward movement of Frémont's massive army. Sigel's advance arrived at the river at Warsaw by October 16, only to find a rickety ferry that would hardly answer to cross thousands of men and wagons over a wide, rising river. The army halted for several days while the Pioneer Corps (engineer troops) worked day and night to complete a bridge. Soon large details of soldiers kept busy cutting down trees to fashion into bridge timbers. Warsaw had been a hotbed of secessionism, and it was from there that the raiders

The Osage River was the only natural obstacle facing Frémont's path to the southwest, but he neglected to provide for a pontoon bridge. The army lingered for several days while engineer troops fashioned timbers and dismantled houses to build a bridge. *Harper's Weekly*

set out to ambush the German Missouri Home Guards at Cole Camp back in July. It was with little compunction, therefore, that the local Southern sympathizers were turned out of their homes to provide quarters for Frémont's officers or that their barns, stables, sheds, and houses were dismantled for additional lumber to complete the bridge across the Osage.

The Pioneer Corps finished the bridge by October 22, and most of Frémont's divisions crossed the Osage. By October 25, the army had moved twenty-five miles south of Warsaw and halted on a large prairie north of Bolivar to allow the scattered divisions to form up for a general advance toward Springfield. Then, with Sigel and Frémont in the advance, the army moved forward to occupy Springfield.

The day before, a report reached headquarters that Springfield was occupied only by a token force of 300 to 400 State Guardsmen. This opportunity was exactly what Maj. Charles Zagonyi wanted. He had commanded a company of Hungarian cavalry in the war against Austria during the Revolution of 1848 and spent two years in an Austrian prison before choosing exile in America. Frémont selected him to form a handpicked bodyguard, a unit that grew quickly to four companies comprising 300 men—all strapping Americans. In a time when there were shortages everywhere, men in the Bodyguard wore regulation cavalry uniforms complete with insignia and yellow trim. Each trooper carried two Colt revolvers and the obligatory saber. The swords were top-quality German steel and construction, made for running through foes during daring cavalry charges. The Bodyguard rode matched bay horses, the finest that could be obtained from the government's stables.

The "kid-glove" brigade soon became the source of popular ridicule and resentment in St. Louis. Frémont's pompous and outsized Bodyguard seemed un-American— more appropriate for the entourage of a king or emperor in some lavish European court than a general of the United States. The soldiers of the Bodyguard had an air of superiority about them that grated on their fellow volunteers as well as taxpaying citizens. The Bodyguard contributed to their leader's isolation by zealously building a wall between their commander and the crowd of citizens who constantly pressed to see him. They assisted in suppressing civil disturbances and arrested citizens who had run afoul of the provost marshal (the late corrupt quartermaster, Justus McKinstry). High-spirited Zagonyi was eager to silence the critics who claimed his pampered men were little more than "Frémont's pets." A glorious military victory would vindicate the Bodyguard and prove its worth and discipline. He begged his commander for the chance to sweep down on Springfield and clean out the nest of Rebels occupying the town.

Hungarian-born Maj. Charles Zagonyi led an elite cavalry unit constituted as Frémont's Bodyguard. Zagonyi yearned to prove wrong those who ridiculed the Bodyguard as "kid-glove" soldiers. *Library of Congress*

With Frémont's blessing, Zagonyi and around 160 of his men left camp after dark on the evening of October 24. They rode toward Springfield, fifty-five miles to the south, where they were to link up with Maj. Frank White and his command of 154 "Prairie Scouts" who had reconnoitered the area. Nine days earlier, White, an energetic twenty-one-year-old New Yorker, had thundered into Lexington with his men, scattering the Rebel garrison and briefly taking possession of the town. He captured a number of prisoners, some supplies and provisions, and also liberated fifteen Union officers who had been held prisoner since the Battle of Lexington, placing them on a St. Louis-bound steamboat that he had also recaptured. White's raiders then galloped out of town before the State Guardsmen could rally and counterattack. With White was a company of Irish Dragoons, commanded by Capt. Patrick Naughton, that arrived too late to join Col. James Mulligan's brigade at Lexington prior to the battle.

Riding throughout the night, Major Zagonyi caught up with the Prairie Scouts near Springfield in the morning. The Hungarian cavalryman assumed command of both units—about 300 men. As they neared Springfield, the riders happened upon a party of State Guard foragers helping themselves to wheat from a barn and

At the time the Civil War broke out, Gen. James H. McBride was serving as a circuit court judge for Texas County. Gov. Claiborne Jackson appointed him a brigadier general of the Seventh Division of the Missouri State Guard, and he went on to lead his Guardsmen in the battles of Wilson's Creek and Lexington. *Used by permission, State Historical Society of Missouri, Columbia*

managed to capture all but one. Zagonyi learned from his prisoners and from local Unionists that Springfield had been reoccupied by Gen. James H. McBride's Seventh Division of the State Guard. Actually, McBride himself was absent, and the part of the division present consisted of newly recruited troops. About 1,000 of these men were encamped west of Springfield; only a few hundred were actually in the town proper. The numerical imbalance daunted Zagonyi not at all. During the Revolution of 1848, he had led a cavalry charge on an Austrian artillery battery and lost more than half his men. He was not about to turn back now and expose the Bodyguard to more ridicule from his commanding general's many critics. He still thought it was possible to damage the enemy by a lightning raid and concluded that any victory, even if devoid of strategic results, would be worth the sacrifice of lives if it proved the honor and courage of Frémont's Bodyguard beyond all doubt. But the forager who escaped capture would certainly alert the Guardsmen in Springfield that a Federal force was bearing down on them. Zagonyi's only hope for surprising the enemy was to approach the town from an unexpected direction. A local Unionist offered to act as guide and showed Zagonyi a detour that might place him in the enemy's rear. Accordingly, the Union cavalrymen left the main road from Bolivar to Springfield and followed a circuitous route to Mount Vernon Road, which approached Springfield from the west.

Major White did not accompany Zagonyi. Hard days of campaigning had left him weak and exhausted. After a few hours of rest, he followed after the command in a carriage, but Zagonyi had not informed him of the change in route. White rode straight into a State Guard picket post and was captured. Meanwhile, Zagonyi approached the outskirts of Springfield where McBride's forces were encamped. They knew he was coming by then and had formed up on an open slope of a hill with a grove of trees to their backs. To reach the base of the hill on which the State Guard forces were formed and launch a charge, Zagonyi's command had to ride down a narrow lane bordered by a rail fence, cross a stream (the head of Wilson's Creek), and form up for the charge. They were outnumbered and would be exposed to enemy fire as they made their way down the narrow lane and crossed the creek. As it turned out, this day, October 25, was the seventh anniversary of the Charge of the Light Brigade at Balaclava in the Ukraine during the Crimean War. Later Zagonyi's operation would be compared to that celebrated but suicidal charge. Zagonyi formed his men in columns of fours and then addressed them, offering his American-born troops the choice of fighting for the honor of their commanding general and their country or turning back. None did. He is said to have given them the battle cry: "The Union and Frémont!" With that he gave the order to move out at a quick trot.

The Federal horsemen charged swiftly down the lane, tightly squeezed between the rail fences. As they came within view of the State Guardsmen, they rode into a hail of murderous fire. Horses reeled and men pitched from their saddles. The leading companies managed to emerge from the lane, cross the creek, and reach the protection afforded by the base of the hill. A third company halted and tried to pull down a section of rail fence for an attack on the enemy's flank, but the fire was too heavy. They remounted and raced to join the others. The Irish Dragoons also tried to move through the break in the fence, but intense enemy fire cut down 13 men, including the two officers. More than decimated by their futile attempt, the

Dragoons retreated from the battlefield. The remaining companies of the Prairie Scouts had scant desire to join the mayhem of struggling men and horses in the lane. They also made their exit from the scene of action, evidently intending to try to intercept and block an attempted retreat by the State Guard. They were not heard from again until the next day.

Meanwhile, Major Zagonyi formed up the survivors who had made it through the lane and across the creek. Then he launched his famous charge. The State Guardsmen were formed into a smaller body of cavalry that was deployed near a small grove of trees and a larger contingent of infantry arrayed along the edge of some woods. Zagonyi's saber- and pistol-wielding cavalrymen pitched into both troops at full gallop. The State Guardsmen, who had yet to receive much by way of military training, lost their nerve, turned tail, and scattered ingloriously in every direction. It was now the turn of Zagonyi's men to draw blood. They pursued the fleeing Guardsmen through the streets of Springfield, impaling some and shooting others. When the sporadic shooting stopped, the Bodyguard had driven McBride's small force out of Springfield.

Zagonyi called off further pursuit at dusk, regrouped his men, and led them to the courthouse square. There they raised the flag of the Union over the town—the first time since Lyon had been there back in early August. For the second time in the war, Union soldiers took control of Springfield. But fewer than a hundred of Zagonyi's troopers were still in the saddle. Sixteen members of the Bodyguard lay in pine coffins in the basement of the new courthouse, and another 37 had sustained wounds. The Bodyguard gave better than they got, however, killing at least 23 State Guardsmen. Still, their butcher's bill was frightfully high for a gesture that was done more to make a point than to achieve real military advantage. The casualty

Zagonyi got Frémont's blessing to clean out the Rebels at Springfield. Undaunted by intelligence that McBride's division occupied the town, Zagonyi found an approach to Springfield along Mount Vernon Road. *Frank Leslie's Illustrated Newspaper*

rate, including wounded and dead, for the Bodyguard was nearly 36 percent, not quite matching the 41 percent rate suffered by the Light Brigade but grievous enough by any standard. The battered victors did not linger in Springfield but rode north in the darkness to link up with Sigel. The Bodyguard sacrificed themselves for the glorification of John C. Frémont, who would manage to cling to his tenuous command for only nine more days.

The next morning, the embarrassed Major White, freed from captivity by local Unionist Home Guards, rode into Springfield and took command of the detachment (only 24 men) that remained with wounded soldiers being cared for in the upper floors of the Greene County courthouse, now a hospital. When a Missouri State Guard party showed up under a flag of truce to claim their dead and wounded, White carefully disguised the small size of his force.

The real liberation of Springfield, at least from the point of view of the sizable

Zagonyi formed his men under enemy fire and, with the battle cry "The Union and Frémont," launched a charge that was likened to that of the Light Brigade at Balaclava. Zagonyi's charge drove the enemy from Springfield but at the cost of a third of his men, wounded or dead. *Frank Leslie's Illustrated Newspaper*

Unionist element in town, took place on October 27, when Sigel's divisions entered the town around noon. The seesaw possession of Springfield left many abandoned and looted homes. The leading men of opposing sympathies had already joined the armies or fled the suddenly inhospitable town, leaving a population of mostly old men, women, and children. Loyalists still remaining flew the Stars and Stripes from their windows or waved small flags as Sigel's soldiers marched into town. Some of the troops recognized folks they knew from the previous summer.

The Pathfinder arrived at Springfield the next day and presided over the burials of the slain members of the Bodyguard. Among the long Federal columns now marching into town were Jim Lane and his hard-bitten Kansas border soldiers. With Lane came 200 mounted and armed African Americans. The sight of them was astonishing and novel in a slave state. Within a year, Lane would have such men in uniform and participating actively in a war to secure their own freedom,

despite the fact that this was not yet an official objective of the war. Lincoln would not issue the Emancipation Proclamation until January 1, 1863, but its seeds were already germinating at Springfield. Several blacks accompanying Frémont's staff as servants formed a self-appointed vigilance committee to secure the freedom of the slaves in the neighborhood. According to Dorsheimer, many of the officers and rank-and-file volunteers from free states welcomed them to their camps and found them quite useful: "They serve us with a zeal, which is born of their long-baffled love of liberty."

This premature emancipation flew in the face of assurances given to provisional governor Hamilton Gamble that the army would return slave property to their owners. While many Regular Army officers (who tended to be conservative and elitist) had little sympathy for abolitionism, volunteer soldiers from the upper Midwest and northern states tended to be much more pragmatic. The notion that Missouri's special brand of Civil War included a commitment to protect the human property of slaveholders did not sit well with soldiers from the free states. Some of the German troops may have been philosophical abolitionists, but the majority were "practical abolitionists" by virtue of the fact that they risked their lives in Missouri and would combat a relentless foe by whatever means necessary. One officer wrote, "Is it to be supposed that men who, like the soldiers of the [Bodyguard] ... pursued Rebellion into the very valley and shadow of death, will be solicitous to protect the system which incited their enemies to that fearful struggle, and hurried their comrades to early graves?"

It would take a much more ghastly valley of death at Antietam to bring the rest of the nation to this insight, but it was already present in Frémont's army, as Dorsheimer noted: "So long as General Frémont is in command of this department, no person, white or black, will be taken out of our lines into slavery. The flag we follow will be in truth what the nation has proudly called it, a symbol of freedom to all."

When Frémont's army crossed the Osage, Sterling Price had relocated his headquarters from Greenfield to Neosho. Now that the Pathfinder was in Springfield,

Price put his army in motion again. Aware of this movement, the rumor arose among the Federal forces that Price had linked up with McCulloch again and was marching toward Springfield to give battle. In terms of job security for Frémont, an attack by Price and McCulloch would have been the best development possible. Lincoln had already drafted the order relieving the commanding general, and a courier was on his way to deliver it to Frémont in person. The only circumstances Lincoln set for not delivering the order were, Frémont "shall then have, in personal command, fought and won a battle, or shall then be actually in a battle, or shall then be in the immediate presence of the enemy in expectation of a battle."

When the Federals learned that Price had his army on the march, they assumed it was because Price knew that only Sigel's division had reached Springfield and that it was, therefore, a ripe target for attack. For two tense days, the troops kept their horses saddled and baggage packed; for two tense nights, the soldiers slept with weapons at hand. If Price attacked, they were prepared to defend the city at extreme cost. They breathed easier when Pope's division arrived on November 1. Frémont now counted 22,000 infantry, 4,000 cavalry, and 70 cannons.

The next day a captain rode to the Pathfinder's headquarters and presented him with his removal orders. Hunter was to succeed him temporarily, but the general had not yet arrived in Springfield. The latest rumors had Price and McCulloch concentrating at Wilson's Creek, only twenty miles away; a major battle seemed imminent. At the urgent pleading of some of his officers, Frémont stated that if Hunter did not arrive by midnight, he would lead the army forward at daybreak. It was all wishful thinking. Price was not headed toward Springfield; indeed, he was headed in the opposite direction toward the Arkansas border.

It turned out that Frémont's grand Army of the West was never unleashed to attack an enemy, and that enemy was nowhere close to Wilson's Creek. How Frémont could have been so entirely ignorant of Price's movements is something of a mystery because he had been in communication with Price and had even had time to cobble together a potentially disastrous joint proclamation with him.

The crossroads city of Springfield was the critical position for all of southwestern Missouri. It had been in Rebel hands since Wilson's Creek and would be turned over to them again when Union forces withdrew after Frémont's removal from command. *Harper's Weekly*

The Frémont-Price Agreement was almost a reprise of the ill-fated Price-Harney Agreement that had caused so much consternation for Blair and Lyon earlier in the year. The first stipulation of this strange document was that both commanders agreed that no arrests would be made within the state of Missouri for the expression of political opinions; the second stipulation stated that all peaceably disposed citizens who had been driven from their homes could return and receive the protection of both armies; the third stipulation proclaimed that all bodies of armed men not recognized by Price or Frémont were ordered to disband at once. Like that with Harney, Price's agreement with Frémont came to naught.

On November 2, General Hunter finally arrived at 11 p.m. and the transfer of command was officially consummated. The change in command was immediately detectable. Hunter called off the planned movement of the army toward Wilson's Creek, and he repudiated the Frémont-Price agreement. As he shortly explained to Gen. Lorenzo Thomas, it would have been "impolitic in the highest degree" to have ratified such an agreement. It would have been impossible to enforce martial law in the state and would have given "absolute liberty to the propagandists of treason." The agreement would have also given "perfect immunity" to disbanded soldiers of Price's command to winter at home before rejoining Price when the campaigning season began the following spring. Since the Unionist Home Guards had not been officially recognized by an act of Congress, their organizations would have been illegal under the agreement. On the other hand, there would be no protection for loyal citizens from guerrilla bands, for they "cared as little for conventions and proclamations as for the Sermon on the Mount."

Frémont's removal caused much distress in the ranks among soldiers who felt that their commander had been removed on the eve of a decisive battle. Many officers (especially among the Germans, who feared loss of influence) threatened to resign their commissions in protest, and some of the troops expressed mutinous sentiments during the episode. In the end, Frémont did the right thing by quelling such talk and issuing a farewell to his troops. When he departed for St. Louis, only his devoted Bodyguard and, oddly, a contingent of Delaware Indians, accompanied him.

Glowing descriptions and engravings of Zagonyi's Charge appeared in *Leslie's* and *Harper's* weekly newspapers, but the Bodyguard's reception back in St. Louis was anything but a hero's welcome. Because the unit had not been organized in accordance with army regulations, the cavalrymen were denied rations and forage and obligated to wear the same uniforms (now quite tattered) they had fought in at Springfield. On November 28, by order of George B. McClellan, who had replaced Winfield Scott as commanding general of the army, the Bodyguard was disbanded without pay. It was cruel treatment for a group that had produced a rare military victory (such as it was) in this bleak period for the Union.

Frémont and his family took up residence in New York City. He still retained strong support among the radical faction, and Lincoln felt pressured to offer him another command—this time the Mountain Department in West Virginia, a position created just to appease the Pathfinder and his friends. There he turned in a mediocre performance in an inconclusive battle with Stonewall Jackson at Cross Keys on June 8, 1862. At the end of the month, after just four months in the Mountain Department, he resigned from the army upon learning that his command was to be incorporated into a newly established Army of Virginia. The new commander turned out to be a subordinate who had done little to help him during his one hundred days in Missouri—none other than John Pope, fresh from his "post-Frémont" Missouri triumphs at Milford, New Madrid, and Island No. Ten.

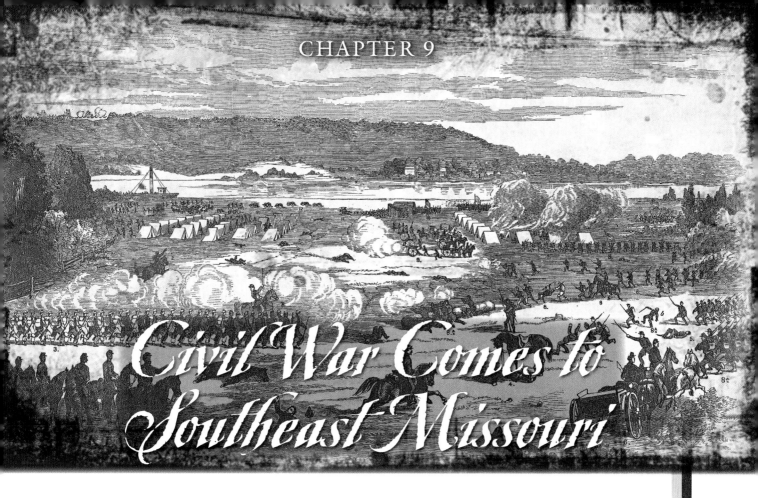

CHAPTER 9

Civil War Comes to Southeast Missouri

RÉMONT NEVER GAVE UP designs on the Mississippi Valley even as he launched his ponderous offensive against Sterling Price in western Missouri. Central to all his plans was to keep Confederates east of the Mississippi River from crossing over and cooperating with the Missouri State Guard. Gen. M. Jeff Thompson's operations in southeastern Missouri grew irritating enough in September 1861 that Frémont assigned Gen. Ulysses S. Grant to command the region and tasked him with destroying Thompson's swamp brigade. Grant commanded much larger Federal forces at Ironton, Cape Girardeau, Bird's Point, and Cairo but was unenthusiastic about the prospects of chasing Thompson, who was without fixed headquarters and equally at home in the swamps of Arkansas as Missouri. His first attempt to catch fleet-footed Thompson had aborted when Union commanders in the field could not agree on who would lead their combined forces.

Grant, like Frémont, looked to the inland waterways, believing them far more strategically promising than operations in the swamps. He used the time wisely by probing down the Mississippi by land and by boat, making the invaluable acquaintance of Cmdr. Henry Walke of the U. S. Navy's Mississippi River gunboat squadron. Both Grant and Walke learned how to combine army and naval assets for riverine offensives.

Confederate Gen. Leonidas Polk gave them an opportunity to exercise their newfound amphibious capability on September 4, 1861, when he violated Kentucky's neutrality by seizing Columbus, the best spot below St. Louis for blockading the Mississippi. The small town was on the high side of the river at the Iron Banks, as the Kentucky bluffs were called. Columbus was the northern terminus of the Mobile & Ohio Railroad and overlooked a ferry crossing to Belmont, Missouri. Polk's engineers and soldiers proceeded to build a "Gibraltar" along the river with a tiered series of forts mounting 120 heavy guns. To hold

The fortress at Columbus, Kentucky, was too strong for Gen. Ulysses S. Grant to attack, so he turned to Belmont, Missouri, on the opposite shore. *Frank Leslie's Illustrated Newspaper*

Ulysses S. Grant was a down-on-his-luck former army officer when the war began. He received his first star as general while stationed at Ironton, Missouri. *Library of Congress*

M. Jeff Thompson got the attention of Union authorities when his Guardsmen captured the Illinois garrison of the Big River railroad bridge and burned the span. Grant sent two columns to deal with Thompson's Swamp Brigade, resulting in the battle at Fredericktown. *Rossiter Johnson, "Campfire and Battlefield," New York: Bryan, Taylor & Co., 1894*

Maj. Gen. Leonidas Polk, a friend of Jefferson Davis, had been an Episcopal bishop before the war. He destroyed the status quo when he violated Kentucky's neutrality and seized the commanding heights at Columbus. *Used by permission, State Historical Society of Missouri, Columbia*

back Yankee gunboats while defending gunners drew their beads, the Confederates stretched a great iron chain across the river and deployed floating mines.

The Lincoln administration had carefully observed Kentucky's declared neutrality, as had the Confederacy, to that point. Polk's action destroyed the status quo. He then allowed Grant to trump him strategically two days later by occupying Paducah, Kentucky, with a river-borne force from Cairo. Grant thereby controlled the mouth of the Tennessee River.

Grant might not have laid a glove on Thompson had General Frémont not become obsessed that Thompson actually shielded Confederate troops crossing from Columbus by way of the ferry to Belmont, Missouri. Then, in mid-October, Thompson and 500 cavalrymen raided the Iron Mountain Railroad south of St. Louis, capturing a company of Illinois infantry guarding the Big River bridge only forty miles south of the city, driving off a relief force, and burning the span. There was only a handful of casualties on each side, but Thompson captured 58 of the bridge guard. It was a costly blow to the railroad company, and the swamp

Looking south from the confluence, this point where the Ohio River meets the Mississippi was the most strategic objective bordering Missouri in the early days of the war. *Library of Congress*

cavalry reveled in more military equipment (courtesy of a single company of the enemy) than they had ever seen before.

It was a nearly singular coup by Thompson; it was another three years before the Confederates managed to cut the Iron Mountain Railroad again. After tearing up everything along the railroad within reach, Thompson paroled his prisoners after giving them the impression that he had a much larger force, complete with a contingent of American Indians! The cavalry then joined the rest of Thompson's brigade at Fredericktown and scattered a detachment of Indiana cavalry. Thompson now threatened Ironton with almost 1,200 troops. Grant responded immediately, sending columns from Ironton and Cape Girardeau—about 4,500 Missouri, Illinois, and Indiana volunteers with eight cannons—converging on Fredericktown.

Thompson realized the swamp brigade was "in a damned tight spot," and withdrew on October 20 toward Greenville with wagons full of the spoils from the Big River bridge raid and sixteen thousand pounds of lead gathered from Madison County mines. He wisely sent the wagons of lead and plunder ahead but then

The Battle of Fredericktown, October 21, 1861, as sketched on the spot by W. J. Hinchey. *New York Illustrated News, November 11, 1861*

rashly decided the next morning to turn about, march back to Fredericktown, and fight whoever he found. He claimed his men wanted to fight, though most of his infantry had never fired a gun at the enemy. Thompson told his troops that the result inevitably would be a retreat before superior numbers, but he thought they might throw a haymaker first.

Thompson marched Col. Aden Lowe's infantry to the edge of town and placed them in a cornfield along the road to Greenville. The tactical plan was for Lowe's men to ambush the Yankees as they emerged from Fredericktown and then retire to a defensive line manned by the remainder of the brigade. When the Yankees hadn't come out by noon, Thompson grew impatient and had his skirmishers drive in the enemy picket guards. This act provoked a storm of artillery fire directed by Maj. John Schofield, the West Pointer and mathematics professor whose last battle had been as Lyon's adjutant at Wilson's Creek. Thompson had two guns himself and gamely directed counter battery fire at Schofield. The artillery duel lasted until the Union cavalry and infantry emerged from Fredericktown. Lowe's men let the Union infantry come within forty yards before they rose from the corn to deliver a stinging volley from shotguns and country rifles, driving the enemy back in confusion with considerable loss.

This was the time for Lowe's regiment to retire, but Lowe himself lingered too long and was shot dead after having emptied his revolver at the enemy. His men broke to the rear, and the center of Thompson's line threatened to give way under renewed artillery fire. Thompson lost one of his own precious artillery pieces when the horses spooked and ran away, forcing abandonment of the gun. His infantry repulsed a cavalry charge before Thompson retreated toward Greenville. Col. Joseph Plummer, commanding the combined Union force, chased Thompson in a six-mile running skirmish before giving up pursuit. Depending on whose account is believed, Plummer either routed the Missourians or Thompson withdrew in good order, ambushing the Yankees several times and repelling several assaults on the rear guard.

It seems that Thompson might have been caught and destroyed on the road to Greenville, but Union commanders again had squabbled in the field. Col. William P. Carlin, "exhausted and sick," left his command to Colonel Plummer, who considered the primary mission, the protection of Ironton, accomplished. He reported only 6 killed and 70 wounded of his own and claimed to have buried over 150 of Thompson's men and captured 80 others along with the cannons. Plummer, however, vastly overestimated the size of the enemy force at 4,000 men. Thompson, in turn, reported that he killed 400 of the enemy, far more than the Union admitted. He rued the loss of Colonel Lowe, the highest-ranking officer of the Missouri State Guard killed under his command, but admitted far less loss and claimed his own army was in better shape than ever. He labeled the campaign by his "little band of heroes" a victory despite the retreat, writing, "I have been a gainer in everything by the fight."

In truth, Fredericktown was about the last significant action by Thompson's First Division of the Missouri State Guard, which began to dwindle due to expiration of enlistment, disease, and desertion. The Big River-Fredericktown campaign had also been a missed opportunity. It was purely a Missouri State Guard affair; Thompson's Confederate allies never advanced to his support at a time when he believed they could have taken Ironton "in an hour." Much to his disgust, the Confederates in Arkansas showed more discretion than valor. Fredericktown was the biggest fight yet in southeastern Missouri, but neither side gained much advantage. The swamp brigade's campaign had not diverted General Frémont from General Price; Thompson's command survived potential disaster and had some material gains but ended up at Bloomfield on the edge of the sheltering swamps, impotent in the face of Yankee aggressiveness and numbers. The citizens of Fredericktown were the biggest losers of the battle. Some of Plummer's soldiers, believing that the townspeople had cooperated in setting up Thompson's ambush, burned eight dwellings and looted the courthouse and Catholic church before leaving. Their commander offered no excuses for the actions of his men, nor did he prosecute the arsonists.

Once Frémont took the field against General Price's army, he directed Grant to advance from Cairo down the Mississippi River toward the Confederate fortress at Columbus, keeping the enemy distracted and preventing any cooperation with Price in Missouri. Grant commanded approximately 20,000 men in his department and got most of them underway in three separate operations. He sent yet another Missouri expedition led by Col. Richard J. Oglesby inland via Commerce and Sikeston against Jeff Thompson, while his troops at Paducah feinted overland toward Columbus. Grant himself put 3,000 men (mostly in untested Illinois and Iowa units) aboard four steamboats at Cairo and headed downriver in company with two gunboats on November 5.

Grant wrote in his memoirs that he set off from Cairo without a preconceived plan or any notion of battle, but his men were so elated at the prospect of battle that he doubted that he could maintain discipline if they didn't get to fight. Like Thompson had at Fredericktown, Grant claimed to have yielded to the aggressiveness of his troops. Then one of Frémont's spies reported that the Confederates were crossing troops into Missouri at Belmont, presumably to overwhelm Oglesby's column, which forced Grant's hand. Most historians believe Grant intended to attack

Col. Joseph Plummer commanded the combined Federal forces at Fredericktown. Depending on the source, he either routed Thompson's forces, or the Missourians withdrew in good order. *National Archives*

Col. Richard J. Oglesby led operations from Commerce and Sikeston designed to draw attention from Gen. Ulysses S. Grant's expedition. *Library of Congress*

somewhere all along. Columbus was too powerful, which left Belmont, Missouri, opposite the Mississippi from Columbus, as an option to attack.

Belmont was barely a village, consisting of two or three dwellings and a few cornfields cut from the primeval forest on the Missouri side of the Columbus-Belmont ferry. There was a small force of Tennessee and Arkansas troops at Camp Johnston (named after Albert Sydney Johnston, the Confederate commander in the West) in a clearing next to the river above the ferry crossing. The encampment, surrounded by felled timber as obstructions, was in sight of General Polk and his staff atop fortress Columbus. Polk never divined Grant's intention but sent Gen. Gideon Pillow and reinforcements across the river when he learned the Union expedition had left Cairo, increasing the number of Confederates at Camp Johnston to 2,500.

As Polk and Pillow watched for Grant from their river bluff positions, Grant landed his troops at a cornfield a few miles above Belmont, just out of sight and out of range of the artillery at Columbus. Leaving a guard with the boats, Grant took his main force through the forest toward Camp Johnston. Confederate resistance increased as the Yankees neared the camp, but Grant's mobile field artillery supported his attack and outgunned the enemy. Gideon Pillow blundered to Grant's advantage by ordering a brave but foolish bayonet attack across open ground while the Union advance was still sheltered in the forest. The result was predictable, and Pillow's men suffered greatly before breaking for the river's edge. Grant's troops were now within range of Confederate siege guns at Columbus, but the artillerists at the fortress withheld fire, fearful of hitting their own men. The next advance took

The *Tyler* and *Lexington* were converted side-wheel steamboats refitted into "timberclad" gunboats in mid-1861 at Cincinnati and were the first gunboats of the Western Gunboat Flotilla. *"Battles and Leaders of the Civil War, Vol. 1"*

the Yankees into Camp Johnston.

At this point, Grant lost control of his exuberant army. The men celebrated prematurely, wandering through the captured tents searching for souvenirs. Politicians among the officers (the most prominent being John A. McClernand, an Illinois war Democrat appointed brigadier general by Lincoln) raced from group to group, delivering speeches with an eye toward the next election, not the enemy. By the time Grant reached the riverbank, the Confederate survivors were working their way upstream toward his transports, and he could see "two steamers, coming from the Columbus side towards the west shore, above us black—or gray—with soldiers from boiler-deck to roof."

The Confederates had four steamers tied up on the river when Grant arrived. Two were tied up empty on the Missouri side, but the other two (those seen by Grant) ferried across Louisiana and Tennessee reinforcements from Columbus led by Col. Ben Cheatham, who organized a counterattack from the Belmont landing. No longer afraid of hitting their own men, Confederate artillerists across the river at Columbus began shelling the Yankees in Camp Johnston. Pillow meanwhile reorganized his command on the banks of the river and menaced Grant's transports.

As Cheatham and Pillow threatened to cut off and envelop Grant's expeditionary force, some of the general's subordinates wanted to surrender. Grant merely ordered the enemy encampment put to the torch, had his buglers blow the signal for "surrounded," and ordered the men to cut their way out back the way they came. A fierce counterblow against Cheatham gave the Union troops time to disengage, but they encountered heavy resistance on the road back to the boats as the Confederates stalked them through the woods. Grant rode ahead to alert his rear guard but to his dismay found

Gen. Ulysses S. Grant's assault on the Confederate encampment at Camp Johnston went well initially but nearly ended in disaster when the men celebrated their victory prematurely. In the meantime, the Confederates rushed reinforcements across the river from Columbus to Belmont and threatened to cut off Grant's men from their transports. *Used by permission, State Historical Society of Missouri, Columbia*

An Illinois War Democrat, John A. McClernand received his commission as brigadier general from Abraham Lincoln. Grant was unimpressed with McClernand at Belmont and ultimately relieved him from high command during the Vicksburg campaign. *Library of Congress*

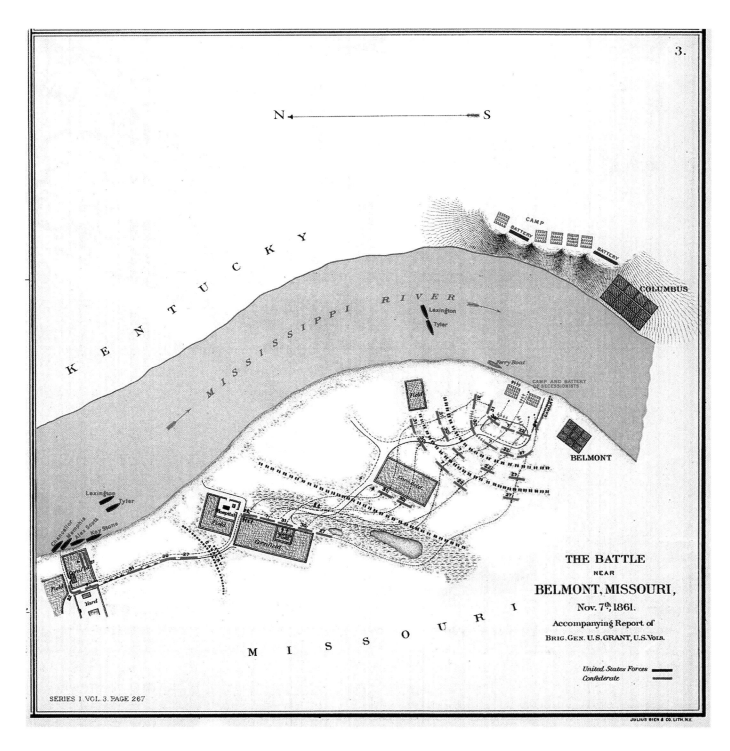

N ← → S

KENTUCKY

MISSISSIPPI RIVER

CAMP
BATTERY
BATTERY

COLUMBUS

Lexington
Tyler

Ferry Boat

CAMP AND BATTERY
OF SECESSIONISTS

Field

CAVALRY

Cornfield

BELMONT

Lexington
Tyler

Chancellor
Memphis
Alex Scott
Key Stone

Hospital
Field

Cornfield

Wood

THE BATTLE
NEAR
BELMONT, MISSOURI,
Nov. 7th, 1861.
Accompanying Report of
BRIG. GEN. U. S. GRANT, U. S. VOLS.

Field
Yard

M I S S O U R I

United States Forces ———
Confederate ————

SERIES I. VOL. 3. PAGE 267

JULIUS BIEN & CO. LITH. N.Y.

Gen. Ulysses S. Grant landed his men above the village of Belmont, where a bend in the Mississippi shielded his landing from the Confederates at Columbus. General Polk learned of Grant's whereabouts when Union soldiers emerged from the forest and attacked Camp Johnston. *Atlas to Accompany the Official Records of the Union and Confederate Armies*

that they had already returned to the transports. The Yankees reembarked under heavy pressure and kept the enemy back with volleys by the infantry and artillery, augmented by naval fire from the gunboats.

Grant rode out for a last look and found himself the last Union soldier between the enemy and the boats as the transports began to back away from the bank. Luckily for Grant, one of the steamboat pilots saw Grant and waited. Grant wrote that "my horse seemed to take in the situation ... put his forefeet over the bank without hesitation or urging, and with his hind feet well under him, slid down the bank and trotted aboard the boat, some twelve or fifteen feet away, over a single gangplank."

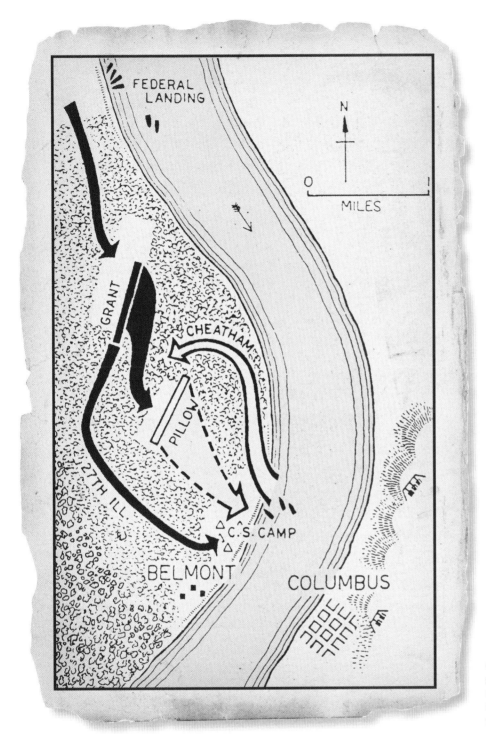

Grant's forces overran Camp Johnston in full sight of the observers at Columbus. When the Confederates ferried troops across the river, Grant's men had to fight their way back to their boats. *Map by William Fannin*

As the boat struggled to back away, Confederate infantry peered over the bank and peppered the transports with rifle fire. The gunboats punctuated the end of the Battle of Belmont with sheets of canister and grapeshot. The navy provided one other signal service, stopping on the return to Cairo to pick up the last of Grant's men—a few hundred infantry and cavalry who had gotten separated from the main force and floundered through the woods before reaching the riverbank above Grant's landing place, where the flotilla found them.

Belmont was a Confederate victory but an inconclusive battle. Both armies sustained about equal numbers of casualties (about 600 each, with more than 100 dead on each side), but the Yankees lost about 20 percent of its force versus General Polk's 16 percent. The Yankees also abandoned their dead and wounded, as well as the battlefield, to the enemy. Both sides could claim some success, Grant for his initial attack and Pillow and Cheatham on the counterattack. As had been usual in 1861, the inexperienced rank and file generally fought well, but their commanders fumbled tactically and showed lapses of judgment under pressure. Generals Polk and Pillow demonstrated their incapacity for command, validating Grant's contempt for their lack of competence (he had seen Gideon Pillow in action during the Mexican War). Grant's boldness on the Mississippi led Polk to strengthen Columbus to the detriment of other parts of his department, most notably in Tennessee.

Northern newspapers castigated Grant for losing a fight that seemed to have no benefit. However, Lincoln recognized in Grant's first Civil War battle an aggressiveness not seen in the west since the late Lyon and was not displeased with his neophyte general. And there were other important benefits to the Union not readily apparent after Belmont. Grant's army was now bloodied and jubilant after their downriver raid. Grant himself gained confidence in the men and his own leadership. Lincoln and Grant ultimately formed the strongest political-military combination of the entire war. Grant left Missouri for the Tennessee River in February 1862. His first great triumphs at Fort Henry on the Tennessee River and Fort Donelson on the Cumberland River collapsed the Confederate defensive line from eastern Tennessee to the Mississippi. The Union victory rendered Columbus untenable, and the fortress turned out to be more Maginot than Gibraltar. Polk's Confederates removed the artillery to other forts downstream and abandoned the position on the Mississippi without a shot.

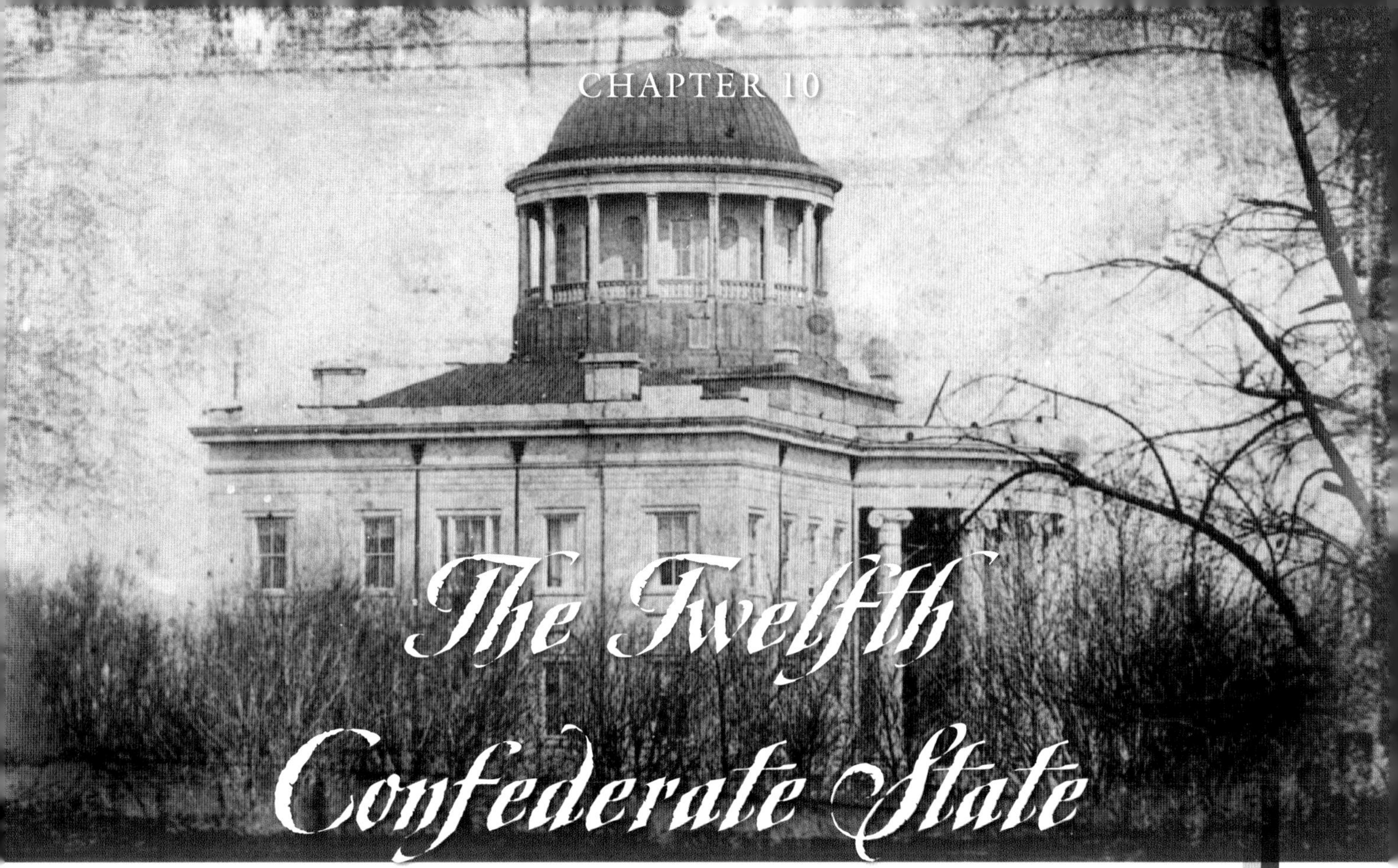

CHAPTER 10

The Twelfth Confederate State

While a provisional Union government in Jefferson City had been directing affairs of state since late July, as summer gave way to fall, there was still no formal alliance between deposed governor Claiborne Jackson's government-in-exile and the Confederate States of America. *Missouri State Archives*

BY MID-OCTOBER, as Frémont's massive army had crossed the Osage and was advancing toward Springfield, Maj. Gen. Sterling Price directed his army to move from Greenville to Neosho, fifty miles south of Springfield. In addition to keeping a good distance between his army and the Federal force slowly advancing toward him, Price hoped to protect the vital lead deposits near Granby, where mining operations were providing two hundred thousand pounds of lead a month for the Southern cause.

Another compelling need was to end the state of political limbo in which the Missouri Southern faction remained mired. The elected executive branch, a portion of the elected legislature, and the State Guard created by these bodies were in a state of war with the United States government and carrying on this war on their own hook. As summer gave way to fall, there was still no formal alliance between Claiborne Jackson's government and the Confederate States of America. Jackson's government had been deposed by the very State Convention that he had caused to be created. This same convention, which had rejected the option of secession, met in late July to create a new state government to take the place of the one that had been elected in 1860. After ousting Jackson, the convention set up a provisional government to work hand-in-glove with the Lincoln administration to keep Missouri solidly in the Union column and to marshal soldiers and resources for the war against secession.

While members of the State Convention met in Jefferson City to unseat Jackson and launch the provisional government, Jackson himself was in Richmond conferring with Confederate President Jefferson Davis. Prior to this meeting, Davis had been reluctant to aid Missouri until the state had formally seceded from the Union. After meeting with Jackson, he softened his position to the extent of promising money to pay the State Guard troops as soon as the Confederate Congress could appropriate

Thomas L. Snead, as an aide to Governor Jackson and adjutant to Sterling Price, personally witnessed and participated in some of the most dramatic events of the first year of the Civil War in Missouri. He later became a Confederate congressman from Missouri. *Missouri Historical Society, St. Louis*

such funds. In addition, Confederate troops from Arkansas and Louisiana had assisted the Missouri State Guard in gaining the significant victory at the Battle of Wilson's Creek on August 10, 1861.

The State Guard's victory at Lexington on September 18-20 had boosted morale on the home front and made Maj. Gen. Sterling Price a popular hero throughout the South. But the gains—recruits attracted to the cause and arms and equipment captured from the enemy—were only short term. It was clear that regaining control of the state would take a much larger military force than Missouri's Southern leaders could muster on their own. Price and Jackson still promoted a Confederate invasion into Missouri to wrest the state from Union domination, but despite success at Lexington, Jackson lacked any kind of formal military alliance with the Confederacy.

To remedy this situation, he dispatched Thomas L. Snead and E. C. Cabell to Richmond to negotiate an offensive and defensive treaty. At the same time, Jackson issued a call from Lexington for the General Assembly to meet in special session at Neosho on October 21, 1861.

A few days later, the Confederate Congress in Richmond, Virginia, passed an act authorizing President Davis to cooperate with Jackson by offering the use of Confederate troops. It also recognized the Jackson government as legally constituted with authority to ratify the Confederate constitution. Once this ratification was accomplished, Missouri could be admitted into the Confederacy on an equal footing with the eleven other seceded states. At Neosho, Jackson would have to assemble a legislative body with enough legitimacy to constitute the "legally elected and regularly constituted Government of the State of Missouri."

The members of the General Assembly who arrived on October 21, 1861, were fugitives liable to arrest. They had to slip through enemy lines to make it to Neosho, and they waited for a week for enough members to constitute a quorum. Finally, on October 28, the members present decided to proceed with business, quorum or not. The session kicked off with a resounding proclamation by Governor Jackson, who accused federal authorities of waging a ruthless war on the people of the state. He argued that the tyrannized citizens were justified in abandoning peaceful means in order to secure their constitutional rights. "War now exists between the state of Missouri and the federal government," Jackson thundered, "and a state of war is incompatible with the continuance of our union with that government."

After Jackson's address and upon his recommendation, the assembly took the momentous first steps toward forging a new destiny for Missouri as part of the Confederate States of America. The legislators met in Neosho for a single day, but during that time, they passed an Ordinance of Secession and then voted to adopt the Provisional Constitution of the Confederate States of America. Although the gesture came late, perhaps too late, the assembly finally gave Jackson the drastic action for which he had hoped since becoming governor in early 1861.

After the day's business, the "Rebel legislature" adjourned to meet on October 31 at the courthouse in Cassville, where Price was shifting his army to put more distance between himself and Frémont, who had just occupied Springfield. Most of the legislative business of the session was transacted at Cassville under the protection of Price's army. The assembly passed an act reorganizing the State Guard and creating ten military districts. Another act confirmed the brigadier generals that Jackson had previously appointed to command divisions of the State Guard. A bill was passed appropriating ten million dollars for the defense of the state. As this was

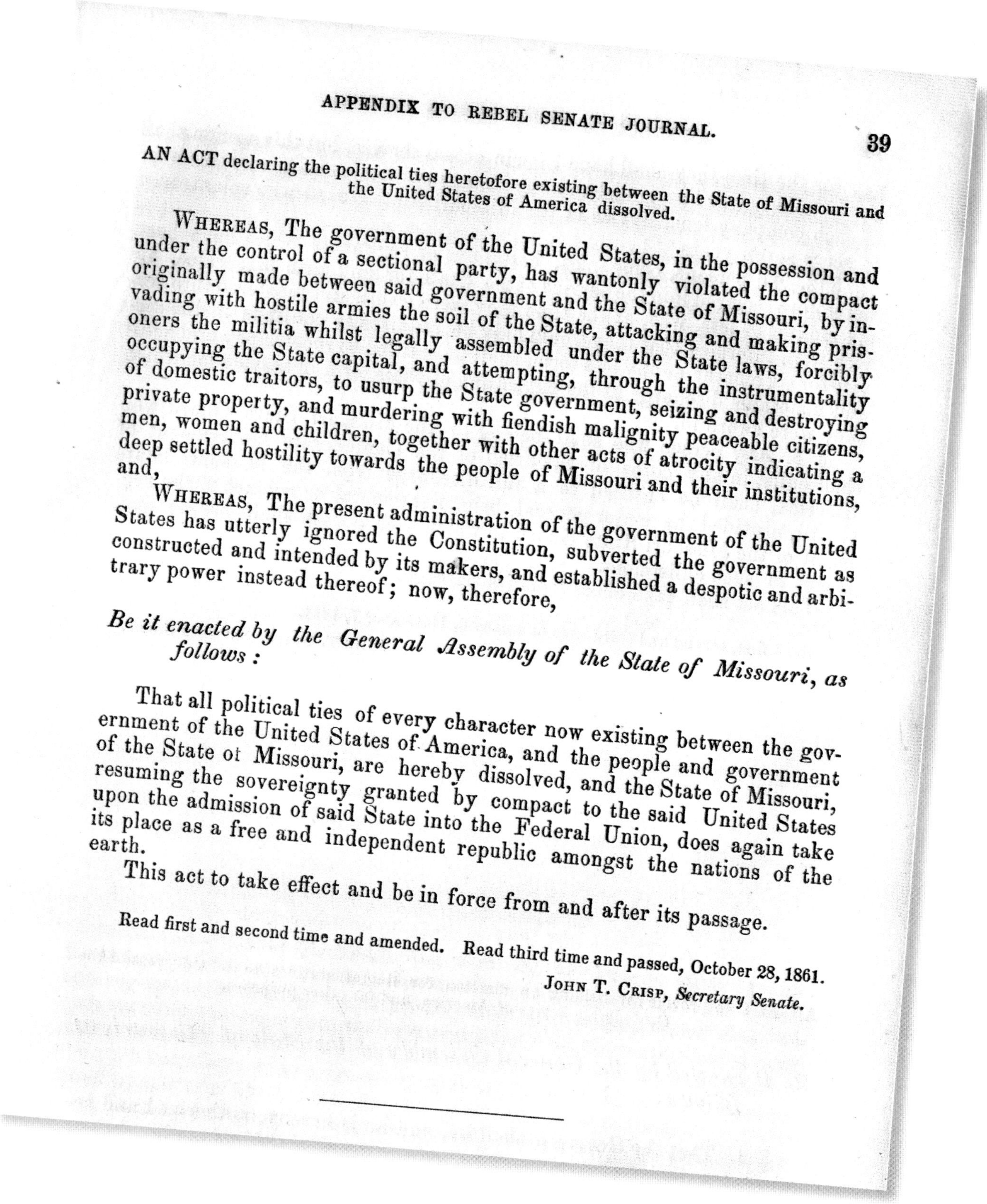

APPENDIX TO REBEL SENATE JOURNAL.

AN ACT declaring the political ties heretofore existing between the State of Missouri and the United States of America dissolved.

WHEREAS, The government of the United States, in the possession and under the control of a sectional party, has wantonly violated the compact originally made between said government and the State of Missouri, by invading with hostile armies the soil of the State, attacking and making prisoners the militia whilst legally assembled under the State laws, forcibly occupying the State capital, and attempting, through the instrumentality of domestic traitors, to usurp the State government, seizing and destroying private property, and murdering with fiendish malignity peaceable citizens, men, women and children, together with other acts of atrocity indicating a deep settled hostility towards the people of Missouri and their institutions, and,

WHEREAS, The present administration of the government of the United States has utterly ignored the Constitution, subverted the government as constructed and intended by its makers, and established a despotic and arbitrary power instead thereof; now, therefore,

Be it enacted by the General Assembly of the State of Missouri, as follows :

That all political ties of every character now existing between the government of the United States of America, and the people and government of the State of Missouri, are hereby dissolved, and the State of Missouri, resuming the sovereignty granted by compact to the said United States upon the admission of said State into the Federal Union, does again take its place as a free and independent republic amongst the nations of the earth.

This act to take effect and be in force from and after its passage.

Read first and second time and amended. Read third time and passed, October 28, 1861.

JOHN T. CRISP, Secretary Senate.

On October 28, 1861, fugitive legislators, driven from the state capital in July by Federal forces, gathered in Neosho and passed an Ordinance of Secession, which declared, "That all political ties of every character now existing between the government of the United States of America, and the people and government of the State of Missouri, are hereby dissolved…" *"Journal of the Senate, Extra Session of the Rebel Legislature called together by a proclamation of C. F. Jackson,"* Published in Jefferson City by Emory S. Foster, Public Printer, 1865-66, Missouri State Archives

The Barry County courthouse at Cassville as it appeared around the time of the Civil War. The "Rebel legislature" met here from October 31 to November 7, 1861, to take the steps necessary to make Missouri a member of the Confederate States of America.
Used by permission, State Historical Society of Missouri, Columbia

money the assembly didn't have, Governor Jackson was authorized to raise this sum through the issuance of defense bonds.

One controversial action taken by the legislature provided for the selection of representatives to the Confederate Congress. The assembly named two senators and seven representatives to serve until an election could be held. This slate was then forwarded to Jackson for his approval. Governor Jackson, ever the strict legalist, reluctantly signed this bill. He knew that neither he nor the assembly had the constitutional authority to appoint representatives. Under the state constitution, these offices were determined by popular election in the case of representatives, or, in the instance of the senators, selected by the state House of Representatives without the consent of the governor. As it was, no elections could be held in Missouri due to the Union occupation. The nine congressmen and their replacements served without a mandate from the electorate in the Confederate Congress for the remainder of its existence.

On November 3, 1861, Governor Jackson signed the Ordinance of Secession and the bill ratifying the Confederate Constitution and forwarded both to Richmond. The assembly adjourned on November 7, after resolving to meet in New Madrid on the first Monday in March 1862. By that time, however, New Madrid was under military siege, and only a handful of representatives managed to show up. No other session of the General Assembly was ever held.

No official record of the members present at the session of the "Rebel legislature"

The secession convention at Cassville appropriated ten million dollars for the defense of Missouri. Since this was money the assembly didn't have, they authorized Governor Jackson to raise the sum by printing defense bonds and paper money.
John Viessman Collection

119

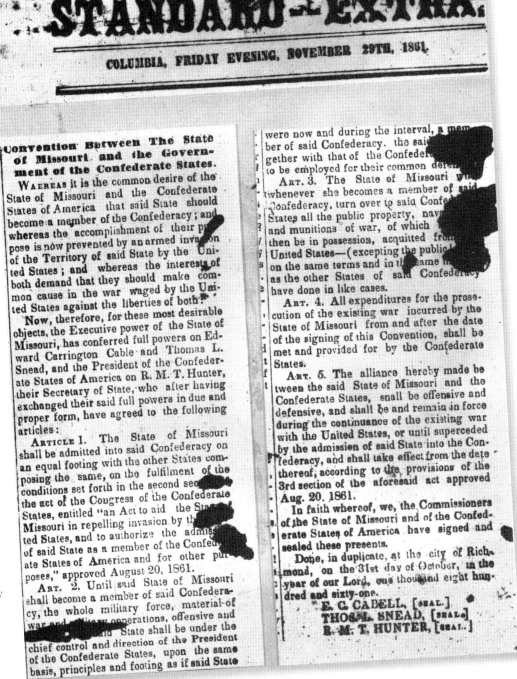

STANDARD-EXTRA.

COLUMBIA, FRIDAY EVENING, NOVEMBER 29TH, 1861.

Convention Between The State of Missouri and the Government of the Confederate States.

WHEREAS it is the common desire of the State of Missouri and the Confederate States of America that said State should become a member of the Confederacy; and whereas the accomplishment of their purpose is now prevented by an armed invasion of the Territory of said State by the United States; and whereas the interests of both demand that they should make common cause in the war waged by the United States against the liberties of both:

Now, therefore, for these most desirable objects, the Executive power of the State of Missouri, has conferred full powers on Edward Carrington Cable and Thomas L. Snead, and the President of the Confederate States of America on R. M. T. Hunter, their Secretary of State, who after having exchanged their said full powers in due and proper form, have agreed to the following articles:

ARTICLE 1. The State of Missouri shall be admitted into said Confederacy on an equal footing with the other States composing the same, on the fulfilment of the conditions set forth in the second section the act of the Congress of the Confederate States, entitled "an Act to aid the State of Missouri in repelling invasion by the United States, and to authorize the admission of said State as a member of the Confederate States of America and for other purposes," approved August 20, 1861.

ART. 2. Until said State of Missouri shall become a member of said Confederacy, the whole military force, material of war and military operations, offensive and defensive, said State shall be under the chief control and direction of the President of the Confederate States, upon the same basis, principles and footing as if said State

were now and during the interval, a member of said Confederacy. the said together with that of the Confederacy to be employed for their common defence.

ART. 3. The State of Missouri whenever she becomes a member of said Confederacy, turn over to said Confederate States all the public property, naval and munitions of war, of which then be in possession, acquitted from United States—(excepting the public on the same terms and in the same as the other States of said Confederacy have done in like cases.

ART. 4. All expenditures for the prosecution of the existing war incurred by the State of Missouri from and after the date of the signing of this Convention, shall be met and provided for by the Confederate States.

ART. 5. The alliance hereby made between the said State of Missouri and the Confederate States, shall be offensive and defensive, and shall be and remain in force during the continuance of the existing war with the United States, or until superceded by the admission of said State into the Confederacy, and shall take effect from the date thereof; according to the provisions of the 3rd section of the aforesaid act approved Aug. 20, 1861.

In faith whereof, we, the Commissioners of the State of Missouri and of the Confederate States of America have signed and sealed these presents.

Done, in duplicate, at the city of Richmond, on the 31st day of October, in the year of our Lord, one thousand eight hundred and sixty-one.

E. C. CABELL, [SEAL.]
THOS. L. SNEAD, [SEAL.]
R. M. T. HUNTER, [SEAL.]

Although Missouri was now the twelfth Confederate state, this was a bittersweet moment because this recognition came too late to have any real effect on Union control of Missouri. *"Convention between the State of Missouri and the Government of the Confederate States," used by permission, State Historical Society of Missouri, Columbia*

is known to exist, nor did the Senate Journal list a roll call of the votes cast. Only sixteen senators and four representatives are mentioned by name in the proceedings of the meeting, leading naturally to a suspicion that a quorum did not exist. Although various Southern newspapers stated that the proceedings were entirely legal, at least one attendee, Isaac N. Shambaugh of Dekalb County, claimed in January 1862 that the meeting was attended at most by eleven senators and forty-four representatives, a number well short of the twenty-seven senators and seventy-seven representatives required for a quorum. He frankly stated, "It need scarcely be added that all the pretended legislation at either place was a fraud, and not only upon the state, but upon the government of the

Confederate States, as well as the United States."

But none of these points of order mattered any more than objections to the legitimacy of the method by which the Unionist Provisional Government was created. What mattered for both governing bodies was official recognition and support from the respective national governments to whom they appealed. For Jackson and his allies, this came on November 28, 1861, when the Confederate Congress passed the act admitting Missouri as the twelfth state in the Confederacy. It was a bittersweet moment. As it turned out, this recognition came too late to have any real effect on Union control of Missouri. One Southern newspaper, the *Charleston Mercury*, stated, "The great state of Missouri is now in the Confederacy. She and the other frontier states are paying the bitter penalty of indecision and trusting Yankee faith."

Historian William R. Geise described the unusual situation that now prevailed in Missouri: "From July 1861 until the end of the Civil War, there were two governments of Missouri. One, sitting in the regular state capitol at Jefferson City, was created under the stress of wartime necessity by a state convention, exercising vague and extraordinary powers. The other, composed of a number of the last regularly elected members of the old state government, became a fugitive government, dispossessed of both capital and state, moving from place to place. … Eventually this shadow government had little claim to legality in Missouri beyond its possession of the official state seal and its recognition by the Confederate States, but for some thirty thousand Missourians who 'went South' it was, for four years, the state executive."

While the exiled legislature was busy laying the groundwork for joining Missouri to the Confederacy, Maj. Gen. Sterling Price attempted to sell his grand strategy for winning back Missouri to any high Confederate official who would listen. While still at Neosho, he wrote to Brig. Gen. Benjamin McCulloch and laid out an ambitious proposal to combine their respective forces for another foray north to the Missouri River. McCulloch had wanted to lay waste to Kansas, but Price argued that this would be futile as long as men and supplies in large numbers could be transported from the East along the Hannibal and St. Joseph Railroad. If this vital cross-state corridor could be destroyed, the enemy would be unable to supply and reinforce their outposts in western Missouri and eastern Kansas. Once the Confederates established themselves in central Missouri, they would receive abundant supplies from citizens grateful for liberation from the yoke of federal tyranny, and volunteers would rush forward to swell the army to 50,000 or more.

This seemed to be an odd plan to be proposing at a time when a Federal army of more than 38,000 soldiers was bearing down on his position. And McCulloch, with his low regard for Price's military abilities, would have nothing to do with such an extravagant and unrealistic proposal. Price was hardly daunted. Far from seeing the advance of Frémont's army as a dire threat from which he would have to flee or face certain annihilation, he saw it as yet another ripe chance to launch a Confederate invasion into Missouri.

The western Confederacy now had a new theater commander, Maj. Gen. Albert Sidney Johnston. He had received this appointment on September 10 from Jefferson Davis, who had known and idolized Johnston since their student days together at Transylvania University in Kentucky. Price quickly wrote to the new commander

Maj. Gen. Albert Sidney Johnston became the ranking Confederate general in the western theater. Gen. Sterling Price attempted to persuade Johnston to open a major front in Missouri by attacking St. Louis, but Johnston had no enthusiasm for this plan because he had his hands full trying to man a defensive line extending from Columbus, Kentucky, to the Cumberland Gap. *Library of Congress*

that the vital stronghold of St. Louis was virtually defenseless because most of the military forces in Missouri had been funneled into Frémont's massive army, which was now far away in the southwest section of the state. When Johnston did not leap at this suggestion to attack St. Louis, Price wrote to him again with more emphasis. He now knew that Frémont had 40,000 men with him and that St. Louis surely had few defenders: "To an officer, general, of your age, large experience, and well-known military sagacity, the bare suggestion of the fact reveals its great importance. ... Is it not the day and the hour to hasten a movement on Saint Louis, the possession of which is of such vast importance to the South?"

Such a movement would require Frémont to hasten back to St. Louis. Price and McCulloch could then join forces and harry the Federal retreat. The bluecoats would be trapped between two enemy forces, and their capture would be certain. Johnston discreetly declined to comment on Price's suggestion: "Of my own plan of operations I can of course say nothing in a letter, for fear it may fall into improper hands." Price's strategic thinking did not extend beyond redeeming Missouri. He hardly acknowledged and perhaps did not comprehend the overwhelming problems facing Johnston, who was attempting to cobble together a defensive line extending from Columbus, Kentucky, through Bowling Green to the Cumberland Gap. Johnston had too few men to cover this widespread front and faced an enemy with greater resources in both manpower and supplies.

Undeterred by the lack of a satisfactory response from the general, Price directed his next appeal directly to President Jefferson Davis. He opened his communication to the Confederate president with a description of the treachery of that summer's Missouri State Convention and the resulting overrunning of the state by Federal forces. Price did not mention that he had been the chairman of the convention. Loyal Southerners had been forced to flee with but few arms or materials of war and little chance to recruit an army. He stated that he now had 12,000 men, all armed and ready to fight, despite the lack of adequate food and clothing. He had withdrawn to the extreme southwest corner of the state to secure needed ammunition and supplies and to link up with McCulloch.

He went on to report that 40,000 Federals were just two days' march away and that St. Louis could now be taken almost without a battle. "Of this I have more than once advised General Johnston." He then made his oft-repeated plea: "Apart from this suggestion, I beg from the Confederate Government a force sufficient to enable us to cut our way to the Missouri River." He went on to weave his usual grand vision of tens of thousands of recruits flocking to the Confederate banner if this movement could be made. "We can have under the authority of our government 50,000 or 100,000 men as soon as we can be placed in such position as to make our strength available."

Perhaps Missouri could have been a valuable asset to the Southern cause had she been led by capable politicians and generals who had struck early, seized the St. Louis Arsenal, forced through an Ordinance of Secession, and established firm control of the state before the Unionists could react. Instead the opposite had happened. The widespread opinion throughout the South was that timid and indecisive leaders had squandered the golden opportunity. More decisive leadership might have added Missouri to the Confederacy back when the transaction included an entire state, well populated with males of Southern birth or ancestry who were of fighting age. The manpower and bountiful resources of Missouri might have served the Southern cause well, and a front might have been opened on the western flank of Yankeedom.

Instead, the state delivered up to the Confederacy little more than a body of

exiles. Jackson, Price, and their Southern cohorts now approached the Confederacy as orphans and beggars needing more help than they could give in return. It did not help that Davis's first impression of Jackson and Price, formed earlier by news of the Price-Harney Agreement, was of vacillating politicians who talked out of both sides of their mouths and lacked resolve or, in the case of Price, military competence. And it didn't help that McCulloch portrayed Missouri fighters as being little more than an undisciplined mob led by politicians.

What President Davis and General Johnston did need very badly from Missouri were men to fill the ranks and bolster the thin defensive lines east of the Mississippi. But these troops were yet to be seen. Jefferson Davis had been besieged by a stream of constant pleas and embittered accusations from Price and Jackson that the Confederate government had abandoned Missouri. But Davis could and did remind these two officials that they had yet to tender a single regiment of Missourians to the service of the Confederacy.

In the meantime, as the official correspondence proceeded, the movement against St. Louis that Price and his subordinate in southeastern Missouri, Brig. Gen. M. Jeff Thompson, clamored for was rapidly becoming yet another lost opportunity. Generals Gideon Pillow and William Hardee had made bold statements about such a movement but failed to back their rhetoric with actions. With Brig. Gen. Ulysses S. Grant becoming increasingly more active in southeast Missouri, the chance for a Confederate offensive in that sector was now quickly evaporating.

As the year's end approached, it was becoming clear that the Confederate leadership had already tacitly conceded control of Missouri to the enemy. They were in a defensive mode; they wanted to hold on to the territory they already controlled and let the enemy come to them. Once Jackson and Price had failed

As the year's end approached, it was becoming clear that the Confederate government, Confederate President Jefferson Davis and his cabinet, had already tacitly conceded control of Missouri to the enemy. Once Gov. Claiborne Jackson and Gen. Sterling Price had failed to seize their moment, Davis felt that resources just weren't there to liberate Missouri by military force. *Library of Congress*

Following Wilson's Creek, Confederate Secretary of War Judah P. Benjamin finally inquired of Gen. Benjamin McCulloch, who was long on excuses but short on actual fighting, for an explanation as to why he failed to join Price in pursuing the enemy. McCulloch sent more complaints and excuses. *Library of Congress*

to seize their moment, the resources just weren't there to liberate Missouri by military force. This was a bitter pill that neither Price nor Jackson, nor a large host of Missourians, was prepared to swallow.

Despite the derogatory characterizations of the military abilities of Price, no one could deny his willingness to go where the enemy was and give battle. And his men would follow him anywhere. While McCulloch presented a long list of reasons why he could not join forces with Price to carry the war to the enemy, Price headed for the heart of Union-controlled Missouri with anyone who would follow. Price had been instrumental, along with McCulloch, in the victory at Wilson's Creek and victorious, in spite of McCulloch, at Lexington. In these days before the ascendancy of Robert E. Lee and Stonewall Jackson, Price was a genuine hero throughout the South. His morale-boosting victories came at a very welcome time for the South, and he might well have continued to keep things lively in Missouri had McCulloch been willing to join forces with him.

But one of the many bleak points of Confederate operations in the West was the failure of Price and McCulloch to work together to conduct joint military operations in Missouri. McCulloch was unwilling to cooperate with Price in any campaign following the Battle of Wilson's Creek. Price could not persuade McCulloch to join him in the incursion into Missouri that brought the Lexington triumph. Because of their feud, Jefferson Davis faced a real problem in the Trans-Mississippi West. Since the two could obviously not cooperate with each other, Davis needed to find a general who could corral the contentious generals and make them work in harness for the good of the war in the West.

McCulloch's refusal to cooperate with Price prompted the Confederate Secretary of War, Judah Benjamin, to inquire of McCulloch: "I cannot understand why you withdraw your troops instead of pursuing the enemy when his leaders were quarreling and his army separated into parts under different commanders. Send an explanation." McCulloch, who was long on complaints and had done little fighting, predictably sent a long, excuse-filled response that reviewed his entire relationship with Price and portrayed the Missouri leader and his men in the same contemptuous terms he had so often expressed before.

Now, with every expectation that Frémont would shortly advance upon the secessionists with the expressed intention of driving them to Little Rock and Memphis, it was vitally important for Price and McCulloch to unite and prepare a common plan of action. On November 7, Price marched his army of six divisions from Cassville to Pineville to form a junction with McCulloch.

At Pineville the generals had to devise a course of action for dealing with Frémont's anticipated advance. However, as might be expected at this stage of their relationship, Price and McCulloch could not agree upon any point of strategy. If a stand had to be made against Frémont, Price wanted it to be at Pineville in extreme southwest Missouri. He and McCulloch, by his reckoning, could muster 25,000 men to oppose Frémont's 38,789 men. The region around Pineville favored the defense. It was rugged country with broken ground and timber to hinder the progress of an enemy army while artillery tore into its ranks. McCulloch thought this was a shortsighted strategy. Frémont could send his infantry forward but hold back his artillery and supply train. At best, a Southern victory in the rugged Pineville region would turn the Federal infantry back, but it would yield no other strategic benefit.

Instead, McCulloch proposed to fall back sixty miles into the Boston Mountains of Arkansas and hope that the Pathfinder followed. This would stretch Frémont's supply lines to their maximum limits while McCulloch, by withdrawing into Arkansas, moved closer to his depots and could gain additional troops from Texas and the Indian nations. With Price's Missourians, these forces could attack the Federals in a location of their choosing where they would not only defeat the Federals but also capture their artillery train of 120 cannon and the rest of the army's baggage and equipment—lock, stock, and barrel.

If McCulloch had his way, Frémont's path south of Springfield would be through a ruined, burned-out landscape devoid of sustenance for the pursuing enemy. The Texan wanted to burn all mills and storehouses of grain that lay in the Union's path and, in fact, had already implemented his policy in Missouri by sending Col. James McIntosh and two Texas regiments to reconnoiter in the direction of Springfield and destroy all mills and forage on their withdrawal. By the time the first Union soldier set foot south of Springfield, a swath of burnt mills, barns, and stacked grain already lined the road toward Fayetteville. McCulloch vowed to continue this destruction along the whole route to the Boston Mountains and urged Price to pursue the same course on his own line of withdrawal.

The tactics appalled and outraged Price, who protested that the farmers affected by such wanton destruction were mostly loyal Southern men, "Above all, allow me to suggest that burning the mills and laying waste the country is an infliction as grievous as any that could be inflicted by the enemy, and our people could have little choice between being shot and starved to death, involving men, women, and children." Price argued that such a policy would win no friends for the Confederate cause in that region and might well drive the loyal Southern population into the Unionist camp.

McCulloch, who had evinced little regard for Missourians of any stripe, replied that, of course, he regretted having to apply the torch but that there was "little danger of any one starving in a country where full crops have been made and only have the population left to consume it. As for Arkansas, every man who is a patriot and sound Southern man will be the first to put the torch to his own grain or mill rather than have them left to aid the enemy. If he is not a true Southern man, it will only be treating him right to destroy that which he would rather let the enemy have than ourselves."

McCulloch hardly had a monopoly on such reasoning. His ruthless and contradictory logic would have done Gen. John Pope or the Kansas Jayhawkers proud. This kind of thinking came to dominate the conflict in Missouri and explains why large sections of western and southern Missouri became uninhabited wastelands by war's end.

CHAPTER 11

Price Moves North Again

The Otterville entrenchments, constructed at the order of Gen. John Pope in December and January 1861, were never used but still survive to this day. *Reenactment photo, James M. Denny, Missouri Department of Natural Resources*

AS IT TURNED OUT, it didn't matter what strategy was pursued by the bickering Southern generals. The Federal pursuit never materialized; Sterling Price and Benjamin McCulloch never fought John C. Frémont's large army in southwest Missouri. Indeed, the opposite happened. Not only did the Federals decline to pursue Price, they also abandoned Springfield without a fight! Exasperated by Frémont's ponderous and futile campaign and considering the resources it would take to supply a large army through the winter in southwest Missouri, President Abraham Lincoln determined to cut his losses.

He issued a recommendation to the Pathfinder's replacement, Maj. Gen. David Hunter, "As you are not likely to overtake Price, and are in danger of making too long a line from your own base of supplies and reinforcements, that you should give up the pursuit, halt your main army, divide it into two corps of observation, one occupying Sedalia and the other Rolla, the present termini of railroad; then recruit the condition of both corps by reestablishing and improving their discipline and instruction, perfecting their clothing and equipments, and providing less uncomfortable quarters."

Hunter was only too happy to apply a literal interpretation to the orders of his commander in chief. On November 8, he ordered the retrograde movement of the huge army. It never engaged in a major battle despite opposing a numerically inferior enemy. While Lincoln was fully aware of the impossibility of directing a military operation from faraway Washington and was willing to allow considerable discretion to his commander in the field, he nonetheless advanced the grossly incorrect assumption, "The main Rebel army (Price's) west of the Mississippi is believed to have passed Dade County in full retreat upon northwestern Arkansas, leaving Missouri almost freed from the enemy, excepting in the southeast of the state." Hunter should have known better but chose not to avail himself of the

flexibility in action that Lincoln offered.

Because of his decision, all Frémont's gains in territory were cast aside without a fight. The enemy repossessed the entire region, forcing hundreds of Unionist residents who had flooded back into the region expecting the protection of the Federal reoccupation to flee their homes again. Perhaps 4,000 refugees—men, women and children, now homeless—followed the shameful retreat rather than remaining to face the wrath of returning secessionists.

Price scrambled to head north again the moment he learned of the Union retreat. He urged McCulloch to join him in yet another foray to the Missouri River, but the former Texas Ranger was willing to go no farther than Springfield. He aimed only to intercept some straggling Federal supply trains, but the Union army had been gone a week by then. So McCulloch pulled back to Arkansas again and set up winter quarters at Fayetteville and along the Arkansas River. Price, meanwhile, turned his army north for another advance into the heart of "enemy" territory. Marching fifteen to eighteen miles a day, his troops passed through Sarcoxie and then through Dade and Cedar counties. Price's men had last visited the area in late summer. Now the extensive prairies of that region were frost covered in the morning. As November wore on, winter winds began to blow across the flat landscape, biting through the thin clothing and worn-out shoes of Price's steadfast men.

Near the charred ruins of Osceola destroyed two months earlier by Jim Lane, Price halted his army and went into winter camp at the fork of the Osage and Sac rivers. He was just fifty miles from the Federal outpost at Sedalia. Again he appealed to McCulloch to join him, writing that Jayhawkers such as Lane, James

When the huge 38,000-man Federal army retreated from southwest Missouri without a fight, the enemy repossessed the entire region, forcing hundreds of Unionist residents to flee their homes for a second time. Perhaps 4,000 refugees—men, women, and children now homeless—followed the shameful retreat rather than remaining to face the wrath of returning secessionists.
John Bradbury Collection

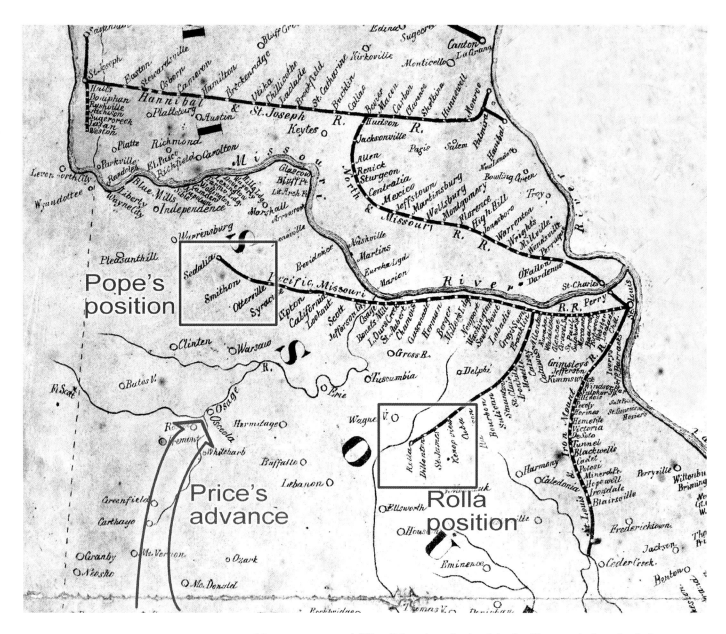

Pope's position

Price's advance

Rolla position

President Lincoln, frustrated with the ineffective campaign against Gen. Sterling Price, told Gen. John Frémont's successor, Gen. David Hunter, "You should give up the pursuit, halt your main army, divide it into two corps of observation, one occupying Sedalia and the other Rolla, the present termini of railroad." The president thought Price was in retreat, but this proved wrong. As soon as the Federals pulled back, Price moved north again. *Detail of Lloyd's Southern Railroad Map, 1863, Library of Congress*

Montgomery, and "Doc" Jennison had spirited off some six hundred slaves, were laying waste to the countryside, and committing barbarous outrages upon the citizenry. Worse, they were preventing thousands of potential recruits from reaching the Missouri army.

By this time, McCulloch was on his way to Richmond, no doubt to cast still more aspersions against Price. The reply was left to his second in command, Col. James McIntosh, who responded in the negative, pleading problems in the Indian territories and the fact that his men lacked sufficient warm clothing to make the long march across cold, bleak Missouri prairies. To another colleague, he intimated that it would be "almost madness" to place forces so close to a well-supplied enemy who could easily concentrate to oppose and defeat any attempted invasion.

As Price would shortly learn for himself, McIntosh was correct. But for the moment, Pap was trying to find a fresh set of ears on which to pitch his usual plea. His last hope seemed to be Maj. Gen. Leonidas Polk, who was then at the Mississippi River "Gibraltar" of Columbus, Kentucky. During the preceding summer, Polk had espoused a strategy very similar to Price's to use the troops of

Pillow, Hardee, Thompson, McCulloch, and Price in a combined assault on St. Louis. Polk evidently dangled this scheme before Price in early December, long after there was any realistic possibility of actually launching such an invasion. But Price leaped at the prospect and promised to deliver 20,000 men (which he didn't have) for a winter campaign against St. Louis.

Price attempted to gather more recruits. On November 26, he published an impassioned plea to the people of central and northern Missouri to step forward: "The foe is still in the field as the country bleeds, and our people groan under the inflictions of a foe marked with all the characteristics of barbarian warfare; and where now are the 50,000 to avenge our wrongs and free our country? Had 50,000 men flocked to our standard with their shot-guns in their hands there would not now be a federal hireling in the State to pollute our soil. ... Where are those 50,000 men? Are Missourians no longer true to themselves? Are they a timid, time-serving, craven race, fit only for subjection to a despot? Awake, my countrymen, to a sense of what constitutes the dignity and true greatness of a free people."

Price also sent officers who had been prominent citizens in central Missouri into counties along the Missouri River to round up recruits. Maybe the answer to Price's taunts was that Missourians truly were a timid and craven race. In any event, they didn't respond to his call. Price's recruiting efforts could only claim limited success. He could tell Polk that 2,500 recruits had come to him from the Lexington area. This was hardly the grandiose army he promised Jefferson Davis and all the other Confederate officials that he had been bombarding with extravagant promises.

In reality, Price's army was not growing—it was shrinking. The six-month enlistments of fully three-fourths of his men were expiring. Although he exhorted his men to reenlist, this time in the Confederate army, most had gone unpaid for their service and were often dressed in little more than rags. They had immediate and pressing concerns to attend to back home. It had been months since they had seen their families, and now that the weather was turning cold, they felt an overwhelming imperative to return to their farms and provide for their loved ones in the face of what looked to be a severe winter. Price had little choice but to grant extended leaves of absence. A few stalwarts did step forward to take the oath and become the first members of the State Guard to enter Confederate service. His army still dwindled. As McIntosh had predicted, Price did not dare to carry on offensive operations against the numerous and well-supplied Union soldiers at nearby Sedalia.

However, the Union high command was initially unaware of Price's straits and credited rumors that he commanded between 10,000 and 30,000 men. They also believed that Price and McCulloch were acting in unison. It never occurred to them that the hardest fighting and most victorious general in the West was held in such low regard by his superiors or that he had received such negligible support from the Confederacy. When Price moved north, they were convinced that another invasion was afoot. But this time, they were determined to make sure that there would be no more disastrous and humiliating defeats, such as Wilson's Creek and Lexington.

By then, the Department of the West had been reorganized into the Department of Missouri and had a new commander, Maj. Gen. Henry W. Halleck. He received his command on November 9, superseding Hunter who had held the departmental command for only a week. Halleck had ranked third in his West Point class of 1839. Bookish and owl-eyed, Halleck had proved to be a competent staff officer during the Mexican War and, as author and translator of treatises on military science, was regarded as the Old Army's intellectual. He had resigned his commission after the Mexican War and made a fortune in California. He had proven a brilliant success

Henry Halleck came back into the United States army after making a fortune in California. Assigned to command the Department of the West, his careful and meticulous administration was a welcome relief to the chaos left by Frémont. *Library of Congress*

as a business executive, railroad builder, and lawyer before being recalled to active duty by Lincoln. His commission as major general dated from August. He acquired a reputation as a careful and meticulous planner with a legalistic cast of mind but ultimately proved to be entirely lacking in the go-for-the-jugular instincts of great field commanders like Grant. But he was a definite improvement over Frémont and fully earned his sobriquet, "Old Brains."

For command of the District of Central Missouri, Halleck selected Brig. Gen. John Pope. Pope could place in the field a force of 15,000 soldiers from Missouri, Iowa, Illinois, Indiana, and other states, and he had forty pieces of artillery and an abundance of transportation and supplies. Pope energetically set about to perfect the defense of the Pacific Railroad, which had been completed as far as Sedalia. At the vital crossing over the Lamine River, near Otterville, he rushed completion of a massive entrenchment capable of holding 3,000 men.

Pope was equally aggressive in sending out large troop detachments to cut off, harass, and capture any potential recruits to the Southern army. In this he produced highly satisfying results. His patrols swept up dozens of the soldiers furloughed by Price, and they provided useful intelligence. By the second week of December, he was able to provide an accurate assessment of the condition of Price's army and the success, or lack thereof, of his recruiting efforts. By December 10, he could report to Halleck's chief of staff that Price was losing men faster than he was gaining them through recruitment and that dissatisfaction within his ranks had resulted in only about half of them signing up for the Confederate army. The rest preferred to remain in the State Guard and in Missouri.

Pope's estimate was that Price probably had no more 4,000 or 5,000 battle-ready

Gen. John Pope perfected the defenses of the Pacific Railroad in central Missouri and, at Milford, smashed recruits trickling to Gen. Sterling Price from northern Missouri. It was a welcome victory after a string of northern defeats. *Library of Congress*

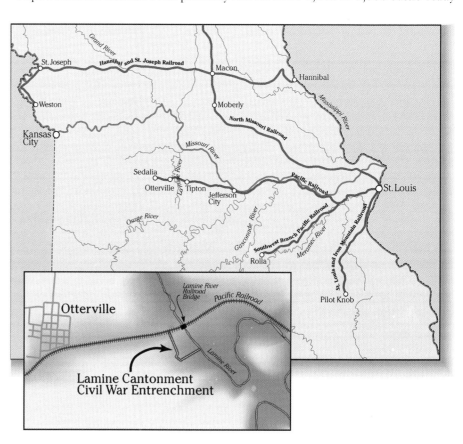

Near the Pacific railhead at Sedalia, Gen. John Pope ordered a massive entrenchment built near Otterville that was capable of holding 3,000 men. The enemy threat, in the form of Gen. Sterling Price, never materialized, and the railroad was never seriously threatened. *Greg Leech and James Denny, Missouri Department of Natural Resources*

130

troops, and most of these were armed only with shotguns. Even if Price's troops were twice this number, he was still badly outnumbered by Pope's better-equipped forces and therefore vulnerable to attack. The Yankee general was convinced that the sooner that Price was dislodged from his Osage River position, the sooner the regions north and south of the Missouri River could be brought under Federal control. He urged Halleck to allow him to conduct an all-out assault on Price and drive him southward.

Halleck, however, was nothing if not extremely cautious. Now, as later, he put the brakes on the aggressive tendencies of his field commanders. He fretted that Price was well supplied with provisions and arms and had a large artillery park. He also was convinced that Price would not retreat without a fight and that his Missourians would rather die than fail to win another victory. He did not think it was possible to strike Price from the rear. A force from Rolla would have to cross the rough terrain of the Gasconade and Osage River hills on difficult roads in frigid weather. A move on his front was equally impractical because of roads and weather.

Additionally, Halleck believed that as many as 10,000 to 15,000 insurgents lingered north of the Missouri River. He feared that if Pope moved on Price, these troops could cross the river and attack his rear. He was also under the impression that 4,000 of the enemy had already crossed the river at Lexington, and he wanted Pope to keep them from forming a junction with Price. All of Halleck's fears were exaggerated. He had no accurate

Gen. Benjamin Prentiss managed to keep the North Missouri Railroad open and the telegraph lines up, despite the persistence of small groups fighting guerrilla-style.
Library of Congress

Union Gen. Jefferson C. Davis was the *other* Jeff Davis of the Civil War. After he failed to come to the relief of the beseiged garrison at Lexington, Davis was instrumental in breaking up the Missouri State Guard camp at Milford.
Library of Congress

assessment of northern Missouri enemy troop strength because his subordinate operating north of the Missouri River, Brig. Gen. Benjamin Prentiss, had been lax about keeping his boss fully informed about enemy activities in his region. This failing would hardly earn him any bonus points from a stickler for protocol like Halleck, who was attempting to micromanage the war in Missouri from St. Louis.

Pope, by a forced march, moved to Clinton. On December 16, he managed to interpose his force between the recruits streaming southward from Lexington and Price's army at Osceola, netting 150 prisoners, sixteen wagons, and other equipment. He soon discovered that the number of recruits numbered not 4,000, but 1,200 at most, and that these men were weaponless, had no supplies, and were dressed in rags. For the next forty-eight hours, two cavalry columns under Maj. L. D. Hubbard and Lt. Col. Egbert B. Brown pursued Price's recruits between Clinton and Papinsville and scattered them in every direction. Hubbard managed to capture an entire company of enemy cavalry along with their tents, baggage, and wagons.

On December 18, Pope got word that another large body of the enemy was moving southward from Arrow Rock and Waverly, headed for camp in the vicinity of Milford in Johnson County. Pope posted the main body of his command to cut off any escape to the south and sent eight cavalry companies, a section of artillery under Col. Jefferson C. Davis, and another regiment of cavalry, Merrill's Horse under Maj. George Marshall, to surround the enemy encampment on both the right and left flanks. Late in the afternoon, Davis ordered a charge across a covered bridge spanning the Blackwater River, surprising the enemy encampment in the wooded bottoms on the west side of the river. Surrounded on all sides, State Guard Col. Franklin S. Robertson had little choice but to surrender or face significant casualties. His troops managed to get off only one volley before turning tail in the face of the Union cavalry charge.

With but two of his soldiers killed, Pope initially claimed to have captured 1,300 men. The actual number turned out to be closer to 684 Guardsmen and a number of civilians. Included were three colonels, one lieutenant colonel, one major, and fifty-one commissioned company officers. The haul also included some five hundred horses and mules, seventy-three wagons loaded with supplies, and about one thousand arms of various kinds. Thirty-four railroad cars were required to transport the prisoners back to St. Louis. One prisoner turned out to be Col. Ebenezer Magoffin, the brother of Kentucky's governor, Beriah Magoffin, and a parole violator. Ordinarily, he would have been marched before a firing squad for this offense, but his family connections earned him a temporary reprieve from Lincoln, who was eager to keep Kentucky in the Union and its governor happy. While awaiting a decision on his death sentence, Magoffin and several other Missourians tunneled under a wall of the military prison at Alton, Illinois, and escaped.

The timing of Pope's victory could not have been better. After an unbroken string of Union military disasters, the triumph at Milford was hailed throughout the North, including a full-page spread in *The New York Times*. Pope became a national hero and ultimately a victim of his own success. His meteoric rise took him from Missouri and lasted only until his inglorious drubbing by Robert E. Lee and Stonewall Jackson at Second Manassas in August 1862.

Operations against insurgents in north Missouri also seemed to be going well. Even after Milford, Halleck remained convinced that there had been upward of 15,000 armed men in that area of the state and that had it not been for the failure of General Prentiss to keep him informed, most of them could have been captured. Despite this failure, Halleck conceded, "The result, however, is satisfactory, as the enemy was completely broken up and deprived of most of his supplies." Prentiss actually had been quite active in dispersing bands of potential recruits north of the

The Alton, Illinois, Federal Military Prison opened on February 9, 1862, and during the next three years housed some 11,764 Confederate prisoners and an assortment of disloyal citizens, including women. Col. Ebenezer Magoffin, brother of the governor of Kentucky, was imprisoned at Alton following his capture at Milford, Missouri. He had been sentenced to death as a parole violator but managed to escape with a number of Missourians by tunneling under the prison wall. *Missouri Historical Society, St. Louis*

133

Missouri River, operating as far west as St. Joseph. He had placed guards along the Hannibal and St. Joseph Railroad to repel bridge burners and to keep the telegraph lines up. Despite the persistence of small parties of armed men who could overpower guards and set fire to bridges, the rail line had been kept open.

By mid-December, Halleck could declare the counties west and north of Brunswick to be cleaned out of Rebels. In central Missouri, Col. Frederick Steele led an expedition through Waverly, Marshall, and Arrow Rock, capturing 50 prisoners, an artillery piece, arms, and wagons of supplies. Three regiments were active in moving against hotbeds of enemy activity in Callaway, Boone, Howard, and Randolph counties. On December 28, Cols. John M. Glover and John W. Birge, each commanding five companies comprising 470 men, moved against a force of some 900 recruits led by State Guard Col. Caleb Dorsey. They encountered Dorsey's men at Mount Zion Church, near Hallsville in Boone County. A hot thirty-minute fight ensued before the superior weaponry of the Federals prevailed. The Southerners quit the field and left their wounded behind. Union troops also captured 90 horses and 105 stands of arms.

Eleven days later, another State Guard recruiter, Col. John A. Poindexter, with a force variously estimated at between 600 and 900 men, was surprised in camp along Silver Creek in northern Boone County at a place called Roan's Tan Yard. A Union cavalry force of 500 swept down upon the camp, and another sharp fight ensued before the green Southerners were scattered. The Union haul was even larger than at Mount Zion, with 160 horses, 60 wagons, 105 tents, 80 kegs of powder, and 200 rifles and shotguns scooped up along with 28 prisoners.

By the third week of December, Price ordered his men to break camp on the Osage River and take up the march for Springfield. It was obvious that there would be no repeat of his triumphal northward march to the Missouri River in September, when western Missouri was nearly free of enemy forces and he could take advantage of the confusion in the Union high command to subdue the garrison at Lexington and linger in the Missouri River country gathering recruits and supplies. Halleck would not repeat Frémont's mistakes. Price succeeded briefly in pinning down a superior Federal force, but that force in turn had foiled his recruiting efforts and was threatening his position.

Price's men spent Christmas setting up winter quarters on the outskirts of Springfield not far from the site of Zagonyi's Charge. There, at a place called Fullbright Spring, his men built relatively warm and comfortable log cabins and even fabricated stove chimneys with bricks from a nearby kiln. The officers, meanwhile, set up quarters in various houses in Springfield. There was still abundant food in the region despite the war. The men dined on turkeys and chickens and even enjoyed fruit pies for dessert. With cajoling from Price and other officers, enough men were persuaded to transfer from the State Guard to Confederate service to form one brigade 2,000 strong—the First Confederate Brigade, commanded by Brig. Gen. Henry Little. A second brigade was also being formed that would be commanded, during the brief amount of life left to him, by William Y. Slack, who would be mortally wounded in battle at Pea Ridge, Arkansas, the following spring. The number of men who signed up was considerably shy of the tens of thousands that Price had promised to Confederate officials. But these men were to prove as fine a group of soldiers as ever fought under the Stars and Bars. The storied First and Second Confederate Brigades were to compile a glorious record in some of the most hard-fought battles of the Civil War. But none of these battles would be in their beloved state. Their dead would lie on many a field of conflict far from their Missouri homes.

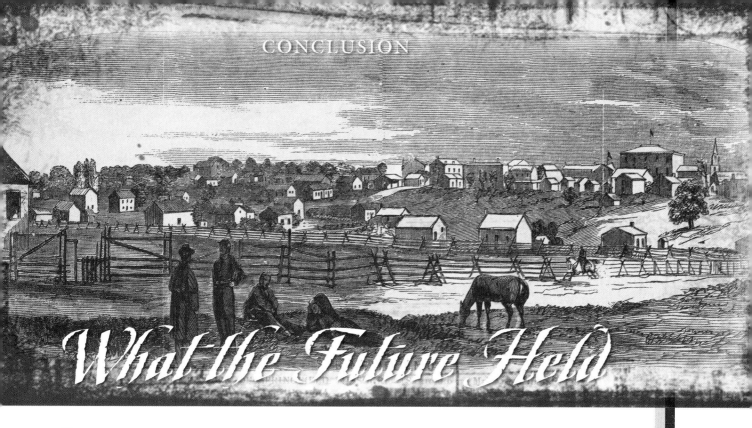

What the Future Held

THE LAST MONTHS of 1861 were halcyon days for Price's long-suffering soldiers. Still unbeaten and with the triumph at Lexington sweet in their memory, Pap's boys for once enjoyed comfortable quarters and abundant rations. But, as they warmed themselves by their fires, even the least contemplative soldiers may have had misgivings at what 1861 had brought them. Their campfires, after all, blazed in military encampments far away from homes and families. The decisive battle and quick conclusion that many had expected when they answered the calls of Jackson and Price were clearly illusory. Despite victories at Wilson's Creek and Lexington and having marched from the Arkansas border to the Missouri River and back, Price's men could claim to control only the southwestern quarter of Missouri.

The enemy held St. Louis, the state's greatest city, as well as its capital, where a provisional administration presumed to take the place of the last duly elected government. Union soldiers and sailors also controlled the railroads and most of the navigable rivers, most notably the Missouri River bisecting the hearthstone of Southern sentiment in the state. For most of Price's men, the worst had already happened: Civil government had collapsed, and their families lived in occupied territory under military repression. No part of the state was spared.

The most politically astute must have realized that the bickering between Jackson, Price, Davis, and McCulloch had already poisoned relations in the new alliance. In any event, Price, as well as Jeff Thompson in southeast Missouri, had seen that their state's best interests were not necessarily those of the Confederacy. In sum, the prospects for 1862 were troublesome for the Missourians' cause, but the men had fought well and were seasoned veterans now. They weren't beaten yet, not by a long shot.

The events of 1861 established the basic parameters of the war in Missouri. Union control of the state's boundaries and most of its resources continued for the remainder of the conflict. Although the federal government occupied Missouri, its control did not extend to the hearts and minds of a sizable segment of the state's population. The differences that had broken up families and neighborhoods had already turned ugly, but the long nightmare of civil discord had only just begun.

Price's men spent Christmas setting up winter quarters on the outskirts of Springfield in warm and comfortable log cabins where they enjoyed an abundance of food. One of Price's officers later recalled: "I am sure that to all Missourians present at the time the winter of 1861-62 passed at Springfield was the best time seen during their military experience." But the comfortable quarters and abundant rations were soon to be exchanged for all the hardships and sufferings incident to an active campaign.
Used by permission, State Historical Society of Missouri, Columbia

Bibliography

BOOKS

The Atlas of the Civil War. Edited by James M. McPherson. New York: Macmillan, 1994. "Clashes in Missouri July 5-November 7, 1861."

Bowman, Dennis K. *Lincoln's Resolute Unionist: Hamilton Gamble, Dred Scott Dissenter and Missouri's Civil War Governor.* Baton Rouge: Louisiana State Press, 2006.

Britton, Wiley. *The Civil War on the Border: A Narrative of Operations in Missouri, Kansas, Arkansas and the Indian Territory During the Years, 1861-62....* New York: G. P. Putnam's Sons, 1899.

Brooksher, William Riley. *Bloody Hill: Civil War Battle of Wilson's Creek.* McLean, VA: Brassey's, 1995.

Brophy, Patrick. *Bushwhackers of the Border: The Civil War Period in Western Missouri: A Summary and Appraisal.* Second, Revised Edition. Nevada, MO: Bushwhacker Museum, Vernon County Historical Society, 2000.

Castel, Albert. *Civil War Kansas: Reaping the Whirlwind.* Lawrence: University Press of Kansas, 1997. Reissue of "A Frontier State at War: Kansas, 1861-1865."

Castel, Albert. *General Sterling Price and the Civil War in the West.* Baton Rouge: Louisiana State University Press, 1968.

Catton, Bruce. *The Coming Fury.* Garden City, N.Y.: Doubleday & Co., Inc., 1961.

Chaffin, Tom. *Pathfinder: John Charles Frémont and the Course of American Empire.* New York: Hill and Wang, 2002.

Cottrell, Steve. *The Battle of Carthage and Carthage in the Civil War.* S.L.: s.n., 1990, 44.

Dempsey, Terrell. *Searching For Jim: Slavery in Sam Clemens's World.* Columbia, MO: University of Missouri Press, 2003.

Denny, James M., *The Battle of Lexington, Sept. 18, 19, 20, 1862.*

Dictionary of Missouri Biography. Edited by Lawrence O. Christensen, William E. Foley, Gary R. Kremer and Kenneth H. Winn. Columbia, MO: University of Missouri Press, 1999.

Etcheson, Nicole. *Bleeding Kansas: Contested Liberty in the Civil War Era.* Lawrence, KS: University Press of Kansas, 2004.

Edom, Clifton C. *Missouri Sketch Book: A Collection of Words and Pictures of the Civil War.* Columbia, MO: Lucas Brothers Publishers, 1963.

Fannin, William. *Defenders of the Border: Missouri's Union Military Organizations in the Civil War.* Jefferson City, MO: Mid-Missouri Genealogical Society, 1982, 21.

Fehrenbacher, Don E. *Slavery, Law, and Politics: The Dred Scott Case in Historical Perspective.* New York: Oxford University Press, 1981.

Fellman, Michael. *Inside War: The Guerrilla Conflict in Missouri During the American Civil War.* New York and Oxford: Oxford University Press, 1989.

Frémont, John C. "Command in Missouri." *Battles and Leaders of the Civil War, From Sumter to Shiloh.* Edited by Robert Underwood Johnson and Clarence Clough Buel. New York: Thomas Yoseloff, 1956.

Gerteis, Louis S. *Civil War St. Louis.* Lawrence, KS: University Press of Kansas, 2001.

Gillespie, Michael L. *The Civil War Battle of Lexington, Missouri: A Concise History of the Siege and Battle, September 12-20, 1861, Based on Eyewitness Accounts* Lone Jack, MO: Author, 1999.

Goodrich, Thomas. *War to the Knife: Bleeding Kansas, 1854-1861.* Mechanicsburg, PA: Stackpole Books, 1998.

Gottschalk, Phil. *In Deadly Earnest: The History of the First Missouri Brigade, CSA.* Columbia, MO: Missouri River Press, Inc., 1991, 562.

Greene, Lorenzo J., Gary R. Kremer, Antonio F. Holland. *Missouri's Black Heritage.* Columbia, MO: University of Missouri Press, 1993.

Harding, James. *Service With the Missouri State Guard: The Memoir of Brigadier General James Harding.* Edited by James E. McGhee. Springfield, MO: Oak Hills Publishers, 2000.

Hinze, David C. and Karen Farnham. *The Battle of Carthage: Border War in Southwest Missouri, July 5,1861.* Campbell, CA: Savas Publishing Company, 1997.

Holcombe, Return Ira, and F. W. Adams, compilers. *An Account of the Battle of Wilson's Creek, or Oak Hills.* Springfield, MO: Dow and Adams, 1883.

Hughes, Nathaniel Cheairs, Jr. *The Battle of Belmont: Grant Strikes South.* Chapel Hill: University of North Carolina Press, 1991.

Hurt, R. Douglas. *Agriculture and Slavery in Missouri's Little Dixie.* Columbia, MO: University of Missouri Press, 1992.

Lenox, David F. *Personal Memoirs of a Missouri Confederate Soldier and His Commentaries on the Race and Liquor Question.* Texarkana, TX: Author, 1906.

McElroy, John. *The Struggle for Missouri.* Washington, DC: National Tribune Company, 1909.

Miles, Kathleen W. *Bitter Ground: The Civil War in Missouri's Golden Valley - Benton, Henry and St. Clair Counties.* Warsaw, MO: The Printery, 1971.

Monaghan, Jay. *Civil War on the Western Border, 1854-1865.* Lincoln and London: University of Nebraska Press, 1955.

Morgan, Jack. *Through American and Irish Wars: The Life and Times of Thomas W. Sweeny.* Dublin: Irish Academic Press, 2005.

Mulligan, James A. "The Siege of Lexington." *Battles and Leaders of the Civil War, From Sumter to Shiloh.* Edited by Robert Underwood Johnson and Clarence Clough Buel. New York: Thomas Yoseloff, 1956.

Parrish, William E. *A History of Missouri, 1860 to 1875.* Columbia, MO: University of Missouri Press, 1973.

Parrish, William E., *Frank Blair: Lincoln's Conservative.* Columbia, MO: University of Missouri Press, 1998.

Parrish, William E., *Turbulent Partnership: Missouri and the Union, 1861-1865.* Columbia, MO: University of Missouri Press, 1963

Parrish, William E., Charles T. Jones, Jr. and Lawrence O. Christensen. *Missouri: The Heart of the Nation.* St. Louis: Forum Press, 1980.

Peckham, James. *Gen. Nathaniel Lyon and Missouri in 1861: A Monograph of the Great Rebellion.* New York: American News Company, 1866.

Peterson, Richard C., James E. McGhee, Kip A. Lindberg, and Keith I. Daleen. *Sterling Price's Lieutenants: A Guide to the Officers and Organization of the Missouri State Guard, 1861-1865.* Shawnee Mission: Two Trails Publishing, 1995.

Phillips, Christopher. *Damned Yankee: The Life of General Nathaniel Lyon.* Columbia, MO: University of Missouri Press, 1990.

Phillips, Christopher. *Missouri's Confederate: Claiborne Fox Jackson and the Creation of Southern Identity in the Border West.* Columbia, MO: University of Missouri Press, 1990.

Piston, William Garrett and Richard W. Hatcher, III. *Wilson's Creek: The Second Battle of the Civil War and the Men Who Fought It.* Chapel Hill: University of North Carolina Press, 2000.

Rombauer, Robert J. *The Union Cause in St. Louis in 1861: An Historical Sketch.* St. Louis: Press of Nixon-Jones Printing Company, 1909.

Rowan, Steven, and James Neal Primm, editors. *Germans for a Free Missouri: Translations From the St. Louis Radical Press, 1857-1862.* Columbia, MO: University of Missouri Press, 1983.

Shalhope, Robert E. *Sterling Price: Portrait of a Southerner.* Columbia, MO: University of Missouri Press, 1971.

Snead, Thomas L. *The Fight for Missouri: From the Election of Lincoln to the Death of Lyon.* New York: Charles Scribner's Sons, 1886.

Starr, Stephen Z. *Jennison's Jayhawkers: A Civil War Cavalry Regiment and Its Commander.* Baton Rouge: Louisiana State University Press, 1973, 1986. Paperback edition, 1993.

Thompson, M. Jeff. *The Civil War Reminiscences of General M. Jeff Thompson.* Edited by Donal J. Stanton, Goodwin F. Berquist and Paul C. Bowers. Dayton, OH: Morningside House, 1988.

Thompson, M. Jeff. *Voices of the Swamp Fox Brigade: Supplemental Letters, Orders and Documents of General M. Jeff Thompson's Command, 1861-1862.* Compiled and Edited by James E. McGhee. Independence, MO: Two Trails, 1999.

Trexler, Harrison Anthony. *Slavery in Missouri, 1804-1865.* "Johns Hopkins University Studies in Historical and Political Science," Series XXXII, No.2. Baltimore: Johns Hopkins Press, 1914.

The War of the Rebellion: A Compilation of the Official Records of the Union and Confederate Armies, Series I--Volume III. Washington: Government Printing Office, 1881.

Ware, Eugene F. *The Lyon Campaign in Missouri: Being a History of the First Iowa Infantry.* Iowa City, IA: Press of the Camp Pope Bookshop, 1991. Reprint of 1907 edition.

Wilkie, Franc B. *Missouri in 1861: The Civil War Letters of Franc B. Wilkie, Newspaper Correspondent.* Edited by Michael E. Banasik. Iowa City, IA: Camp Pope Bookshop, 2002.

Winter, William C. *The Civil War in St. Louis: A Guided Tour.* St. Louis: Missouri Historical Society Press, 1994.

ARTICLES

Anders, Leslie. "'Farthest North': The Historian and the Battle of Athens." *Missouri Historical Review* 69 (January 1975), 147-168.

Anders, Leslie. "The Blackwater Incident." *Missouri Historical Review* 88 (July 1994), 416-429.

Cain, Marvin R. "Edward Bates and Hamilton R. Gamble: A Wartime Partnership." *Missouri Historical Review* 56 (January 1962), 146-155.

Castel, Albert. "Kansas Jayhawking Raids into Western Missouri in 1861." *Missouri Historical Review* 54 (October 1959), 1-11.

Castel, Albert. "The Siege of Lexington." *Civil War Times Illustrated* 8 (August 1969), 4-13.

Chase, Charles Monroe. "A Union Band Director Views Camp Rolla: 1861." Edited by Donald H. Welsh. *Missouri Historical Review* 55 (July 1961), 307-343.

Covington, James W. "The Camp Jackson Affair: 1861." *Missouri Historical Review* 55 (April 1961), 197-212. Illus.

Crisler, Robert M. "Missouri's 'Little Dixie.'" *Missouri Historical Review* 42 (January 1948), 130-139.

Denny, James M. "Civil War Entrenchment Near Otterville." *Boone's Lick Heritage* 7 (June 1999), 4-9.

Dorsheimer, William. "Fremont's Hundred Days in Missouri," I. *Atlantic Monthly* 9 (January 1862), 115-125.

Dorsheimer, William. "Fremont's Hundred Days in Missouri," II. *Atlantic Monthly* 9 (February 1862), 247-258.

Dorsheimer, William. "Fremont's Hundred Days in Missouri," III. *Atlantic Monthly* 9 (March 1862), 372-386.

Dyer, Robert L. "A Closer Look at the Site of the First Battle of Boonville," *Boone's Lick Heritage* 3 (December 1995), 4-9.

Ethier, Eric. "Where Hemp Won the Day." *Civil War Times* 42 (April 2003), 10-11. Battle of Lexington, 18-20 September 1861.

Geise, William R. "Missouri's Confederate Capital in Marshall, Texas." *Missouri Historical Review* 58 (October 1963), 37-54. Illus.

Harvey, Charles M. "Missouri From 1849 to 1861." *Missouri Historical Review* 92 (January 1998), 119-134.

Herklotz, Hildegarde Rose. "Jayhawkers in Missouri, 1858-1863," Part 1. *Missouri Historical Review* 17 (April 1923), 266-284.

Herklotz, Hildegarde Rose. "Jayhawkers in Missouri, 1858-1863," Part 2. *Missouri Historical Review* 17 (July 1923), 505-513.

Herklotz, Hildegarde Rose. "Jayhawkers in Missouri, 1858-1863," Part 3. *Missouri Historical Review* 18 (October 1923), 64-101.

Kirkpatrick, Arthur R. "Admission of Missouri to the Confederacy." *Missouri Historical Review* 55 (July 1961), 366-386.

Kirkpatrick, Arthur R. "Missouri in the Early Months of the Civil War." *Missouri Historical Review* 55 (April 1961), 235-266.

Kirkpatrick, Arthur R. "Missouri on the Eve of the Civil War." *Missouri Historical Review* 55 (January 1961), 99-108.

Kirkpatrick, Arthur R. "Missouri's Delegation in the Confederate Congress." *Civil War History* 5 (March 1959), 188-198.

Kirkpatrick, Arthur Roy. "Missouri's Secessionist Government, 1861-1865." *Missouri Historical Review* 45 (January 1951), 124-137.

Laughlin, Sceva Bright. "Missouri Politics During the Civil War." *Missouri Historical Review* 23 (April 1929), 400-426.

Laughlin, Sceva Bright. "Missouri Politics During the Civil War." *Missouri Historical Review* 23 (July 1929), 583-618.

Laughlin, Sceva Bright. "Missouri Politics During the Civil War." *Missouri Historical Review* 24 (October 1929), 87-113.

Laughlin, Sceva Bright. "Missouri Politics During the Civil War." *Missouri Historical Review* 24 (January 1930), 261-284.

Lindberg, Kip & Jeff Patrick. "In the Shadow of the Light Brigade: The Charge of Frémont's Bodyguard." *North & South* 7 (May 2004), 56-72.

Lyon, William H. "Claiborne Fox Jackson and the Secession Crisis in Missouri." *Missouri Historical Review* 58 (July 1964), 422-441.

McCausland, Susan A. Arnold. "The Battle of Lexington as Seen by a Woman." *Missouri Historical Review* 6 (April 1912), 127-135.

McGhee, James E. "The Neophyte General: U.S. Grant and the Belmont Campaign." *Missouri Historical Review* 67 (July 1973), 465-483.

Merkel, Benjamin G. "The Abolition Aspects of Missouri's Antislavery Controversy 1819-1865." *Missouri Historical Review* 44 (April 1950), 232-253.

Merkel, Benjamin G. "The Slavery Issue and The Political Decline of Thomas Hart Benton, 1846-1856." *Missouri Historical Review* 38 (July 1944), 388-407.

Miller, Robert E. "Zagonyi." *Missouri Historical Review* 76 (January 1982), 174-192. Illus.

Myers, Linda S. and John F. Bradbury, Jr. "On the Road to Wilson's Creek: The Ruination of Samuel C. McCullah." *White River Valley Historical Journal* 44 (Summer 2005), 22-27.

Page, Dave. "A Fight for Missouri." *Civil War Times Illustrated* 34 (July/August 1995), 34-38. Battle at Athens, Mo., 5 August 1861.

Parrish, William E. "David Rice Atchison: 'Faithful Champion of the South.'" *Missouri Historical Review* 51 (January 1957), 113-125. Illus.

Parrish, William E. "General Nathaniel Lyon: A Portrait." *Missouri Historical Review* 49 (October 1954), 1-18.

Patrick, Jeff. "The Battle of Lexington." *North & South* 1 (February 1998), 52-67. Illus.

Phillips, Christopher. "Calculated Confederate: Claiborne Fox Jackson and the Strategy for Secession in Missouri." *Missouri Historical Review* 94 (July 2000), 389-414.

Phillips, Christopher. "The Radical Crusade: Blair, Lyon, and the Advent of the Civil War in Missouri." *Gateway Heritage* 10 (Spring 1990), 22-43.

Phillips, John F. "Hamilton Rowan Gamble and the Provisional Government of Missouri." *Missouri Historical Review* 5 (October 1910), 1-14.

Potter, Marguerite. "Hamilton R. Gamble, Missouri's War Governor." *Missouri Historical Review* 35 (October 1940), 25-71.

Robbins, Peggy. "The Battle of Camp Jackson: Street Fighting in St. Louis." *Civil War Times Illustrated* 20 (June 1981), 34-43.

Rorvig, Paul. "The Significant Skirmish: The Battle of Boonville, June 17, 1861." *Missouri Historical Review* LXXXVI (January 1992), 127-148.

Sigel, Franz. "The Military Operations in Missouri in the Summer and Autumn of 1861." *Missouri Historical Review* 26 (July 1932), 354-367.

Stanton, Donal J., Goodwin F. Berquist, Jr., and Paul C. Bowers. "Missouri's Forgotten General: M. Jeff Thompson and the Civil War." *Missouri Historical Review* 70 (April 1976), 237-258.